BRITISH AIRWAYS

BRITISH AIRWAYS

GÜNTER ENDRES

LONDON

IAN ALLAN LTD

Acknowledgements

In preparing this book, I have been fortunate enough to have had the co-operation of a great many people from both inside and outside British Airways. Their invaluable assistance has been much appreciated.

British Airways

James Croall, Public Affairs Manager
John Silver, Public Affairs Flight Operations and Technical
Ken Cook, Public Affairs
David Gill, Public Affairs
Bernd Wietfeld, Public Affairs Manager Germany
John Lampl, Public Affairs Manager USA
Gerry Devine, Manager Highlands Division
Robert Falkner, Deputy Director Administration
Geoff Bridges, Managing Director Cargo
Geoff Birchall, Senior Cargo Business Manager
John Lavender, Customs Related Superintendent Cargo
John Wiles, Engineering Projects Manager British Aircraft
Stuart Schofield, Production Engineering Manager Wide Body Aircraft
Chas Hipkin, Manager Maintenance Training
Alan Noad, Joint Editor Engineering Magazine
Mike Bannister, Senior First Officer Concorde
Bill Brown, Senior First Officer Concorde
Colin Willis, Cabin Service Director
Kim Lyndon-White, Colour Photo Library
Tara Taylor, Colour Photo Library

British Airways Engine Overhaul

David Williams, Production Engineering Manager
R. G. Martin, Assistant Production Manager

British Airtours/Caledonian Airways

Eamonn Mullaney, Managing Director
Ron Bridge, Flight Support Superintendent
Adrian Hunt, Head of Operations
Brian Bradbury, Engineering Manager
R. M. Davis, Product Delivery Superintendent Catering

also John Stroud, Air Transport Historian, who has provided some excellent information on predecessor companies from his vast store of knowledge, and
Rita Woods, PR Consultants Scotland
Paul Shea, Civil Aviation Authority
Sue Lister, Scott Gold Blyth
Austin J. Brown, Aviation Photographer
Geoffrey P. Jones, Aviation Photographer
Tony Carre, Aviation Photographer
Brian Service, Aviation Photographer
Adrian Meredith, Aviation Photographer
Nick Barralet, British Aerospace
Federica De Luca, Press Officer SAGA
Ian McMahon, Public Affairs Manager Scottish Airports
Ken Perks, Freight Marketing Manager Birmingham International Airport
Richard Schano, Manager PR and External Relations Salzburg Airport
Carol Sigrist, Zurich Airport
Dean Smith, Manager Public Affairs Transport Canada
J. Death, Senior Public Relations Officer, Australian Department of Aviation
Carolyn M. Fennell, Director of Community Relations, Orlando International
Captain Peter J. Howard
Peter Zsille, Aviation Historian Budapest
Ian MacFarlane, Aviation Photographer
Graham Thorneycroft, Royal Air Force Museum

Foreword

For the vast majority of the travelling public, contact with an airline is limited to a visit to a booking office, check-in desk and a flight in one specific aircraft scheduled on a particular service or holiday charter. During such times, travellers may find themselves having to deal with no more than a handful of airline employees, though they will undoubtedly notice a number of others in their immediate surroundings. Not enough perhaps, to stop and wonder what it takes to become and remain the world's favourite airline.

Leaving politics and profit and loss accounts to others, this book is intended to open doors normally closed to outsiders, to allow a glimpse, and it can be no more than that, at a fascinating world beyond. A world of thousands of men, women and machines, each a tiny but important piece of a giant jigsaw, busily striving to knit together the fabric that makes that magic carpet which takes the traveller to the corners of the earth, in hours rather than days, every day and in all weathers. At speeds faster than sound, and yet in safety and comfort.

Günter G. Endres

To my Mother
Who introduced me to the exciting world of aircraft and airlines whilst working for BOAC more than twenty-five years ago
and to all the staff of British Airways,
past, present and future.

Contents

First published 1989

ISBN 0 7110 1734 4

© Günter Endres 1989

Published by Ian Allan Ltd, Shepperton, Surrey; and printed by Ian Allan Printing Ltd at their works at Coombelands in Runnymede, England

1 From Canvas to Concorde – British Airways Yesteryear

It is to George Holt Thomas and **Aircraft Transport and Travel** that credit must go for founding the dynasty which was to grow into today's international flag-carrier known simply as British Airways. 25 August 1919 heralded the bright new dawn of air transport, when a two-seat de Havilland DH16 converted day-bomber left Hounslow Heath, London, bound for Paris-Le Bourget on what is generally regarded as the world's first sustained, scheduled international passenger service. On that inaugural flight, one passenger protected under a 'portmanteau' lid, had to share the tiny cabin with a mixed cargo of mail, grouse and Devonshire cream.

Barely a week had passed before **Handley Page Transport** started a competing service to Paris from London (Cricklewood) using modified Handley Page 0/400

Below
It was left to a man of vision, George Holt Thomas, whose Aircraft Transport and Travel turned destructive war machines to positive use on the world's first passenger service to Paris. The de Havilland DH16 pictured was built from DH.9A components. *British Airways via RAF Museum*

twin-engined bombers from its own factory, and followed it up with a service to Brussels. A third carrier, **S. Instone & Co**., appeared on the Paris route in February 1920, the pride of their fleet being another converted bomber type, the Vickers Vimy. It is interesting to note that, in the summer of 1920, airline operations at London were transferred from Hounslow to Croydon to take advantage of the latter's closer proximity to the continent and, perhaps more pertinently, its location outside the London fog zone.

Against all expectations, these early pioneering services to the continent established a high degree of regularity, but in spite of their undoubted technical skills, the companies found it impossible to make money. The inertia of an unconvinced public and fierce competition from heavily subsidised foreign operators forced fares down from 20 guineas to 6 guineas. Pilots offered to work without pay but even this generous gesture failed to turn the tide.

By the end of February 1921 all services had been suspended, and for a period of 19 days up to 18 March the English air terminal of Croydon was used exclusively by foreign airlines. One permanent casualty was Aircraft Transport and Travel which had suspended services the previous December and failed to come out for round two.

With modest government support, services were resumed in March by Handley Page Transport and S. Instone (later to become **Instone Air Line**) between London and Paris. In April 1922 the two airlines were joined on the London-Paris route by the **Daimler Airway**, which had acquired the assets of Aircraft Transport and Travel, using the new DH34. All three extended their services to other European cities before the route structure was somewhat loosely rationalised with Handley Page concentrating on Paris, Instone on Brussels and Daimler on Amsterdam.

Above:
Other companies quickly followed, among them Handley Page Air Transport with modified 0/400 bombers, and S. Instone & Company with their pride and joy, the Vickers Vimy Commercial pictured here.
British Airways via RAF Museum

Imperial Airways

Whilst the fortunes of the airlines took a turn for the better, subsidies were still not enough to carry them through the difficult winter months and, on 2 January 1923, the Government appointed a Civil Air Transport Subsidies Committee under the Chairmanship of Sir Herbert Hambling to consider the working of the cross-Channel subsidies scheme and to advise on long term solutions. The committee recommended that existing air companies should be welded into one strong organisation charged with the development of external routes. Thus, on 31 March 1924, **Imperial Airways** was born out of the four subsidised British airlines which included Handley Page Transport, Instone Air Line, the Daimler Airway and **British Marine Air Navigation** (which had started a Southampton-Guernsey service with Supermarine Sea Eagle amphibians on 25 September 1923).

The new 'national' airline was floated with a nominal capital of £1million and was granted a total government subsidy of a similar amount to be spread in decreasing

quantities over 10 years, by which time it was hoped that commercial air transport would be self-supporting. Subsidy arrangements were extended in 1928 largely to meet the responsibility of Empire traffic.

Imperial Airways inherited a good deal of traffic on 2,850km of cross-Channel routes together with a motley collection of 18 modified World War 1 aircraft – most of which were obsolete and five unserviceable. The operational fleet comprised three Handley Page W8bs, seven de Havilland DH34s, two Supermarine Sea Eagles and one Vickers Vimy Commercial. The first Imperial Airways service was operated with a DH34 on 26 April 1924 between London and Paris, but from then on further exploitation of European routes became of secondary importance to the principal aim of developing air links with Britain's overseas territories.

The Empire Route to India and Australia
To service Britain's political commitments in the Middle East as a result of the war, the RAF had been operating air mail and courier services between Cairo and Baghdad – the so-called 'Desert Air Mail' – since 23 June 1921. This provided the first step in Imperial Airways' expansion plans eastwards, formalised when agreement was reached with the Air Ministry at the end of 1925 for air services between Egypt and India. Between 10 November 1924 and 17 March 1925, a survey flight was made by Sir W. Sefton Brancker, then Director of Civil Aviation, with Mr (later Sir) Alan Cobham and representatives of Imperial Airways. Landing grounds, meteorological aids, wireless stations and rest houses were built in the

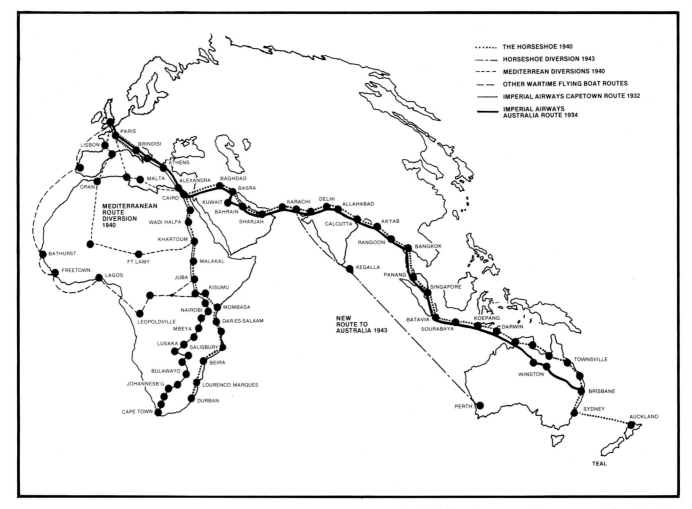

The map legend:
- ········ THE HORSESHOE 1940
- — · — · HORSESHOE DIVERSION 1943
- — — — MEDITERREAN DIVERSIONS 1940
- — — OTHER WARTIME FLYING BOAT ROUTES
- —— IMPERIAL AIRWAYS CAPETOWN ROUTE 1932
- ▬▬▬ IMPERIAL AIRWAYS AUSTRALIA ROUTE 1934

Empire routes 1932–43

wilderness between Amman, Jordan and Ramadi near Baghdad, Iraq, and the first service was operated on 7 January 1927 between Basra and Cairo.

With potentially hostile tribesmen living around Rutbah Wells, Iraq, the station had to be given military protection and a fort was built complete with battlements and towered strongpoints. During construction, nightstop pas-

Below:
The Armstrong Whitworth Atalanta four-engined high-wing monoplane was used on the route to South Africa.
British Airways via RAF Museum

sengers had to live in a tented compound patrolled by guards. Aircraft used on this service were examples of the DH66 biplane, one of the first of the new types ordered by Imperial Airways for Empire passenger and mail traffic.

For over two years the plan to extend the route through Persia and Baluchistan to Karachi was frustrated by the Persian government's refusal to permit aircraft to overfly the country, but the first England-India service eventually left Croydon on 30 March 1929. Only short stages were possible at that time, the whole journey taking seven days. Passengers were flown in an Armstrong-Whitworth Argosy from London to Basle via Paris. Then, because of the refusal of the Italian government to allow British aircraft to enter Italy via France – and flying over the Alps was not yet considered practical – passengers, freight and mail were transferred by train to Genoa. From there, newly-commissioned Short S8 Calcutta flying boats flew to Alexandria via Rome, Naples, Corfu, Athens, Suda Bay (Crete) and Tobruk, and the DH66 Hercules took over on the final sector from Cairo to Karachi, taking in Gaza, Rutbah Wells, Baghdad, Basra, Bushire, Lingeh, Jask and Gwadar.

As the years passed the route was gradually extended eastwards to Calcutta and Rangoon and, on 9 December 1933, Imperial Airways reached Singapore. The dream of an England-Australia service became reality a year later when on 8 December 1934 a weekly mail route was

Above:
In 1922 Daimler Airway, which had acquired the assets of Aircraft Transport and Travel, joined the others on the London-Paris route using the new de Havilland DH34.
British Airways via RAF Museum

opened between London and Brisbane. Handley Page HP42s and Armstrong-Whitworth AW15 Atalanta aircraft were used at first beyond Singapore, until **Qantas Empire Airways** (formed jointly by Imperial and Qantas), substituted DH86s on the route in February 1935. The first passengers from London left Croydon on 13 April 1935 and arrived at Brisbane 12 days later. This 12,700-mile (20,500km) haul was the longest air route in the world.

Below:
Armstrong Whitworth Argosy biplane of Imperial Airways photographed at Khartoum in the Sudan.
British Airways via RAF Museum

Across Africa

With the route to India firmly established, Imperial Airways turned its attention to the second of the main Imperial trunk lines, that of linking Britain with South Africa. As far back as 1919, the RAF had begun preparatory work on behalf of the Air Ministry for van Ryneveld and Brand's flight to the Cape in 1920 in a Vickers Vimy. Establishing airfields across the mountains, jungles and swamps of Central Africa was a tremendous achievement in a continent where firm and level ground suitable for conversion into a landing strip was as elusive as King Solomon's treasure. Most airfields had to be carved by native labour out of dense forests or rocky foothills, or literally squeezed out of mud at the edges of swamps. All this hard work could be washed away in one downpour of tropical rain. At Ndola, Zambia, for instance, the only feasible site was a stretch of ground festooned with anthills

– not the tiny anthills of the English countryside, but solid 12m-diameter pillars as high as telegraph poles. A total of 25,000 tonnes had to be cleared away by hand. Between 16 November 1925 and 13 March 1926, the intrepid Alan Cobham flew from London to Cape Town and back in a de Havilland DH50J, and further survey work by the Air Ministry and Imperial Airways in 1929 led to a regular flying boat service as far as Mwanza on Lake Victoria, opened on 28 February 1931. Mail-only through services to the Cape were started on 20 January 1932 and passengers were carried from 27 April that same year. The service took 11 days and involved 33 stages and six different aircraft, as well as two train journeys. When the famous 'Empire' class flying boats came into service in the late 1930s, the journey was reduced to four-and-a-half days. Services to Britain's territories on the west coast were started on 9 February 1936, involving some more formidable pioneering work across Africa. The service branched off from Khartoum to Kano via Fort Lamy (now Ndjamena) and was progressively extended to Lagos, Accra and Takoradi.

Above:
Imperial Airways' Short 'C' class 'Empire' flying boat, one of 28 of the type in service, added new comfort and cut journey times to Australasia and southern Africa. *Shorts*

Above:
The 'Frobisher' class de Havilland DH91 Albatross, originally intended for transatlantic mail operations, flew Imperial Airways' cross-Channel services in the months before the outbreak of war. It was the first aircraft to carry the 'Speedbird' symbol. The Albatross is seen here at Croydon with the elderly Handley Page HP42W *Heracles*.
British Airways via RAF Museum

The Empire Air Mail Scheme

This ambitious scheme, introduced in 1934 and in full operation by 1938, provided for the automatic carriage of all first class mail by air. It swept away postal surcharges between participating countries and introduced an era when the addition of a standard 1½d British postal stamp to a letter was in itself enough to ensure its carriage by air to almost everywhere within the British Commonwealth.

The Empire Air Mail Scheme was to be a 10-year scheme and included a substantial subsidy for development, as well as guaranteed repayment of all costs for carrying mail. It involved a total annual load of 2,000 tonnes over and above Imperial Airways' existing traffic commitment. This extra commitment highlighted the urgent necessity for new aircraft and, with the consent of the Air Ministry, Imperial Airways took the unprecedented step of ordering 28 Short 'C' class four-engined flying boats – the 'Empire' boats – straight off the drawing board. The first of the type came off the slipway at Rochester on 2 July 1936 and entered service on the trans-Mediterranean route on 30 October that same year. The 'all-up' principle had to be applied progressively as the new boats were delivered and section by section the Empire routes were transformed, offering new standards both in performance and comfort. The Empire boat weighed 18 tonnes and had two decks, one for crews and one for passengers, and a promenade in which they could stretch their legs. It carried 24 passengers at a cruising speed of 144mph (233km/h). By the beginning of 1939, the Imperial 'family' – Imperial Airways with the local operators in the Dominions and Colonies – was flying 24,800 miles (40,000km) a day on European and trunk services over about 28,000 miles (45,000km) of routes. Regular services were in operation to the Middle East, India, Burma, Siam, Singapore, Hong Kong, Australia (in conjunction with Qantas Empire Airways) and to Central, West and South Africa.

The First British Airways

British Airways, backed by Whitehall Securities, was the product of a merger on 30 September 1935 of three domestic operators, **Spartan Air Lines** which had operated its first service on 1 May 1933 between Heston and the Isle of Wight, **United Airways** formed on 4 April 1935 to start services between Heston and Blackpool and the Isle of Man and **Hillman's Airways**. A fourth airline, **British Continental Airways**, operating between Croydon and Amsterdam and Brussels, was absorbed on 1 August 1936.

Hillman's Airways, formed by Edward Hillman – an omnibus operator – had started a service from Romford to Clacton-on-Sea on 1 April 1932 and added a Romford-

Paris service a year later, undercutting Imperial Airways by one-third. He used the DH84 Dragon which he helped to develop as a cheap 'air bus' and from which followed the highly successful DH86 and the DH89 Dragon Rapide.

From the outset, British Airways – now a major carrier – concentrated on Europe. In 1936 it was assisted by an unlikely ally when the Air Ministry was released from its agreement with Imperial Airways not to subsidise any other organisation for air services in Great Britain and Europe, at least as far as services north of a London-Berlin line were concerned. A subsidy of £20,000 was then allotted to British Airways which, on 17 February 1936, pioneered Britain's first excursion into Scandinavia by opening a service to Malmö via Amsterdam, Hamburg and Copenhagen. This was later extended to Stockholm, and British Airways also served Paris and Brussels and provided night mail services to Cologne, Hannover and Berlin using at various times Heston, Gatwick and Croydon as London termini. A lack of suitable British civil aircraft occasioned by the more immediate need to modernise the Royal Air Force, forced British Airways to turn to Fokker F.XIIs for use as first-line equipment. By 1938 it had progressed to the Junkers Ju 52/3m, Lockheed L10 Electra and its bigger sister ship, the L14, often referred to as the Super Electra. With the latter, services were introduced on 17 April 1939 to Budapest via Frankfurt and to Warsaw via Berlin.

British Airways genealogy

Transatlantic Trials

With the commitments of linking the Empire, the development of the Atlantic routes was left almost exclusively to Germany and France, and it was not until 1937 that any serious British attempts were made. Imperial Airways used two specially-equipped Short S30 flying boats, based on the 'Empire' boats, to begin a series of survey flights in July between Southampton, Montreal and New York, via Foynes (Ireland) and Botwood (Newfoundland). These were followed in July 1938 by the short-lived 'pick-a-back' experiment with the Short Mayo composite aircraft *Maia* and *Mercury*, during which *Maia* launched *Mercury* in mid-air with a full load of petrol. The flight between Foynes and Montreal took 20hrs and 20min. Experimental mail services, begun on 5 August 1939, were interrupted by the outbreak of war and had to cease on 30 September.

During that same period British Airways was entrusted with the development of an experimental service to West Africa as a first step in the ultimate establishment of a route to South America. In the autumn of 1937, a party from British Airways and the Air Ministry visited Lisbon and proceeded to West Africa via Casablanca, Las Palmas, Villa Cisneros, Port Etienne and Dakar. In June 1938 ground facilities were surveyed between Natal (Brazil) and Buenos Aires (Argentina) and a series of trial flights were later carried out between London and Lisbon and to Bathurst (now Banjul) in The Gambia. Further development, however, was forestalled by the war and imminent changes in Britain's airline structure.

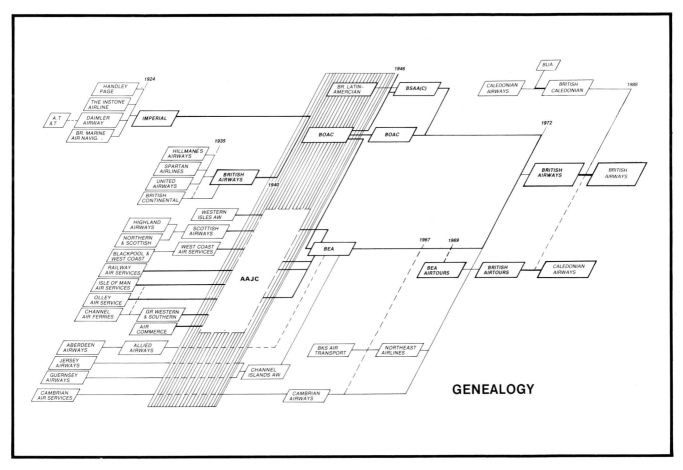

GENEALOGY

11

The Establishment of BOAC

The success of Imperial Airways' long-haul 'Empire' routes could not obscure the fact that it had neglected certain aspects of its European obligations. In November 1937, following trenchant criticisms in a debate on British civil aviation in the House of Commons, a Committee of Enquiry was appointed under the Chairmanship of Lord Cadman.

Among the recommendations in its report, published in March 1938, were that British external air transport should be concentrated in a small number of well-founded and substantial organisations, and that no route should be operated by more than one company to avoid indiscriminate competition. Imperial Airways was to concern itself primarily with the development of Empire and other long-haul routes, with European air services entrusted to British Airways with the exception of the London-Paris route which was to be a joint undertaking. The government accepted in principle that the two airlines should work in separate orbits with little overlap.

For a short time there was a precarious division of spoils but, in November 1938, the government decided to go one step further and amalgamate the two companies into a single public corporation under the title of **British Overseas Airways Corporation (BOAC)**. The corporation was formally established on 24 November 1939 and took over the undertakings of Imperial Airways and British Airways with effect from 1 April 1940.

Warbirds

On 3 September 1939 Britain declared war on Germany and all civil flying ceased. Imperial Airways' and British Airways' aircraft and equipment were placed at the disposal of the Secretary of State for Air. Both companies' land planes were moved from Croydon and Heston to Whitchurch near Bristol, and Imperial Airways' flying boats from Southampton Water to Poole Harbour. Another flying boat base was established later in the war at Foynes, Ireland.

Domestic airlines were united on 5 May 1940 by the formation of the **Associated Airways Joint Committee (AAJC)** following an agreement between the Secretary of State for Air and seven airlines. The seven were **Air Commerce, Great Western and Southern Air Lines, Isle of Man Air Services, Olley Air Service, Scottish Airways, Railway Air Services** and **West Coast Air Services.**

The most influential of these was Railway Air Services (RAS), backed by the 'Big Four' railway companies and Imperial Airways. RAS began operations on 7 May 1934 with a Plymouth-Haldon-Cardiff-Birmingham-Liverpool route, leading to an extensive network of air services throughout southern England with trunk routes through the Midlands to Belfast, Glasgow and the Isle of Man. British Airways continued to serve Scandinavia for a time, re-scheduled from Perth in Scotland, and Armstrong-Whitworth AW27 Ensigns operated the Paris service until

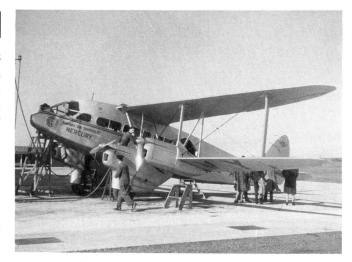

Top:
Railway Air Services built its fleet around the de Havilland biplanes including the DH86 (seen here) which was first delivered in 1934.
John Stroud

Centre:
Anything with wings was put to the BOAC war effort including a large fleet of Lockheed Lodestars used mainly in the Gulf and Africa.
British Airways via RAF Museum

Above:
The long war years left BOAC with a fleet mostly of bomber conversions and the airline had to turn to the United States for more modern equipment which included the Lockheed Constellation, and Boeing Stratocruiser pictured.
BOAC

15 June 1940, that date bringing to an end all services across Europe. The following February, BOAC began its 'ball-bearing' run between Leuchars (Scotland) and Sweden, which was maintained throughout the war using mainly Whitleys and Mosquitos.

Most of the S23 flying boats, later supplemented by Short Sunderlands, were deployed on the vital 'Horseshoe' supply route from Durban to Australia, opened on 19 June 1940. Main points on the route were Lourenco Marques (now Maputo), Beira, Dar-es-Salaam, Mombasa, Kisumu, Khartoum, Cairo, Baghdad, Basra, Karachi, Calcutta, Rangoon, Bangkok and Penang, with Qantas operating the Singapore-Sydney sector. Three newly acquired Boeing 314 flying boats were put on the West African service to Lagos via Lisbon, Las Palmas, Bathurst, Freetown and Takoradi. Trans-African services were also flown. Both BOAC and the AAJC continued to provide all skeleton air services which were an essential part of the total war effort, flying 33 different types of unarmed aircraft in hostile skies and under the most hazardous conditions. In the course of these duties, 81 BOAC staff gave their lives, and casualties among the aircraft fleet were heavy.

Postwar Progress

BOAC emerged from the war covered in glory but ill-equipped to face the challenges ahead. For six long years the country's aircraft industry had been preoccupied with military production and consequently BOAC had to make do at the end of the war with uncompetitive aircraft, mostly bomber conversions such as the Halton and the Lancastrian, with which it resumed its direct England-Australia service on 31 May 1945 in association with Qantas.

Even with a fleet of 175 aircraft, made up of 11 land planes and seven flying boat types, BOAC had to turn to the United States for more modern and competitive equipment. Lockheed L-049 Constellations entered service on a twice-weekly run to New York on 1 July 1946, and Boeing Stratocruisers joined the fleet on 6 December 1949. In the same year BOAC put one of the first British postwar airliners – the Handley Page Hermes – into service, as well as the Canadair C-4 'Argonaut', a Canadian-built Douglas DC-4 with Rolls-Royce engines.

Above:
By the time BEA had taken over all domestic operations, its fleet, then based at Northolt, consisted of 120 aircraft including Junkers Ju52/3ms, Avro 19s, de Havilland Rapides, together with Douglas DC-3s and Vickers Vikings which formed the backbone of the fleet.
British Airways via RAF Museum

The last flying boat was withdrawn from service on 7 November 1950. BOAC's long-haul network then served Australia, Hong Kong, South Africa, Nigeria, Canada, the USA and Bermuda. Routes to South America were added with the absorption of British South American Airways Corporation (BSAAC) on 30 July 1949.

Once peace had returned, BOAC was also rapidly re-establishing its European links; on New Year's Day 1946 it set up a **British European Airways Division** with a fleet of DC-3s based at Northolt, 16 miles west of London. On 4 February BEA took over the continental operations of No 110 Wing of RAF Transport Command, and on 1 August 1946 it became a separate state corporation. At that time BEA served Amsterdam, Brussels, Helsinki, Madrid, Paris and Stockholm, and the introduction of new routes became an almost daily occurrence. The DC-3 remained the backbone of the fleet until supplemented on 1 September by the Vickers Viking, a successful development of the Wellington bomber.

In line with government policy, BEA also took over on 1 February 1947 the services of the domestic airlines which had resumed independent operations after the disbandment of the AAJC, together with others no longer operational. **Channel Islands Airways** and **Allied Airways (Gandar Dower)** came into the fold in April. The aircraft fleet then consisted of 22 DC-3s, 11 ex-Luftwaffe Ju 52/3ms, 29 Vikings, 45 Rapides and 12 Avro 19s, which enabled the airline to tackle with some vigour the expansion of European routes. At the same time some rationalisation of its inherited domestic network was undertaken.

By the time the Airspeed Ambassador (known in BEA service as the Elizabethan) came into service on 13 March 1952, BEA had established itself as a major European airline, a position it maintained and strengthened further still with the introduction one year later of the turboprop

Vickers Viscount which became Britain's most successful postwar airliner. Routes extended throughout Europe and beyond to the Lebanon and North Africa.

British South American Airways Corporation

A third state corporation was established on 1 August 1946 out of **British Latin-American Air Lines**, which had been formed in January 1944 by five shipping companies to head off possible postwar competition, but was incorporated into BOAC on 30 July 1949.

After starting commercial operations on 15 March 1946 between London and Buenos Aires via Lisbon, Bathurst, Natal, Rio de Janeiro and Montevideo, BSAAC concentrated on two principal routes to South America, that to Buenos Aires and to Santiago (Chile) via Bermuda, Jamaica, Venezuela and Peru. Minor changes of routeing were effected over the following years, and a service to Havana, Cuba, branched off from Nassau, Bahamas in August 1948. Unpressurised 13-seat Lancastrians (converted Lancaster bombers) were used at first followed by 21-seat Avro Yorks, which became the mainline aircraft late in 1946. On 31 October 1947, the larger and pressurised Avro Tudor was put on the mid-Atlantic route and was also used extensively – mostly as a tanker – on the Berlin Airlift in the winter of 1948-49. At the end of 1947, BSAAC had experimented with a series of flight refuelling tests between London and Bermuda during which a Lancaster was refuelled by another based in the Azores.

The short history of the airline was colourful but beset by equipment problems throughout. Several accidents, including two mystifying – and to date unexplained – losses of Tudors in the western Atlantic and the 'Bermuda Triangle', contributed greatly to its incorporation into BOAC.

The Coming of the Comet

With the advent of the 1950s, BOAC had its eyes firmly fixed on the de Havilland Comet to put itself and the British aircraft industry back on top. After beginning development flying in early 1951, BOAC began the world's first scheduled passenger service by turbojet when it put the Comet 1 on the London-Johannesburg route on 2 May 1952. For almost two years the Comets operated safely, cutting journey times almost in half on routes to South Africa and the Far East but then disaster struck. On 10 January 1954, a Comet broke-up in mid-air over Elba and within three months a second fell out of the blue sky near Naples in similar circumstances. The most thorough investigation of an aircraft ever undertaken at the Royal Aircraft Establishment (RAE), Farnborough, concluded that metal fatigue had led to a rupture of the fuselage skin, causing instantaneous decompression and the break-up of the aircraft. The Comet disasters dealt a shattering blow to BOAC and Britain who had reached into the unknown and paid the price. With its fleet plans wrecked, BOAC had to cancel its routes to South America and reintroduce aircraft already retired from mainline service. Douglas DC-7Cs also had to be acquired to overcome temporary problems with the new Bristol Britannia four-engined turboprop. When the Britannia finally entered BOAC service on 1 February 1957, jet aircraft were already breathing down its neck. Nevertheless, the 'Whispering Giant' served BOAC well for a number of years. After a gap of four years, the Comet was to reappear as the Comet 4, similar in appearance but much redesigned, enabling BOAC to open the first transatlantic jet service between London

Below:
Even allowing for the disastrous setbacks with the Comet 1, the redesigned Comet 4 still gave BOAC an early lead over its competitors.
British Aerospace

and New York on 4 October 1958, beating all competition. The new Comet became a great success and with the introduction by BEA of the short range Comet 4B in April 1960, traffic increased on many domestic and international routes. Soon more than 60% of BEA's traffic was carried by the Comets and the Vickers Vanguard, which entered service on the corporation's short-haul routes on 22 February 1961.

A Prosperous Period

The early sixties proved a difficult time for all airlines, but the introduction into BEA service of the rear-engined Trident on 1 April 1964, and of the Vickers VC10 on BOAC's West African routes on 29 April that same year, heralded the start of a successful period for both corporations. When the Super VC10s supplemented BOAC's Boeing 707s (in service since 1962) on the New York route in April 1965, they became the envy of all with their outstanding comfort and quietness. The admiration for Britain's latest airliner was unfortunately not translated into many orders from other airlines. After the VC10, BOAC went over almost entirely to American-built aircraft. However, BEA continued to operate British aircraft like the Viscount, Vanguard, Trident and One-Eleven, for many years to come.

In 1967 BEA established **British Air Services** to look after its financial interests in **BKS Air Transport** and **Cambrian Airways**, both of which became wholly-owned subsidiaries in October. BKS (later renamed **Northeast Airlines**) had developed a network serving Newcastle and Leeds/Bradford among others, and Cambrian operated domestic and European schedules radiating mainly from Cardiff, Bristol and Liverpool. A **BEA Airtours** division began operating European inclusive tours on 5 March 1970. A mention must also be made of BEA's helicopter operations which were started as early as 1947 with the setting-up of its **Helicopter Experi-mental Unit**. Night mail services under contract to the Post Office were operated before BEA went on to open the world's first scheduled helicopter service in June 1950 between Liverpool, Wrexham and Cardiff, using 4-seat Sikorsky S-51s. Other routes were tried, but the helicopter was still in a very early stage in its development and success was difficult to come by. In 1964 the Sikorsky S-61 arrived and this led to a highly successful operation between Cornwall and the Scilly Isles, taking over from fixed wing aircraft. By 1979 the service had carried one million passengers. Also in 1964, BEA became the first company to enter the offshore support business when the search for oil and gas began off the East Anglian coast.

Full Circle

In yet another endeavour to bring some sense of order to Britain's air transport – and there have been many – the government appointed a committee under Sir Ronald Edwards in 1967 to consider the future organisation of civil aviation. In its highly acclaimed report published two years later, the committee recommended that BOAC and BEA should remain the principal carriers, but that there should be a 'second force' airline, strengthened by the transfer of BOAC's flag services to West Africa and Libya. This airline was to be British United Airways, which had already taken on BOAC's South American routes in 1964, but its purchase by Caledonian Airways in 1970 handed the mantle of the 'second force' over to British Caledonian Airways.

Below:
The Vickers Viscount and its larger development the Vanguard, both turboprop types much loved by the traveller, helped to keep BEA in the forefront of domestic and European operations.
BEA via Mike Stroud

The 1970 Government White Paper went even further in outlining the complete merger of the two state corporations. Thus on 1 April 1972 **British Airways** came into being when the British Airways Board, set up by the Civil Aviation Act of 1971, assumed control and ownership of the British Overseas Airways Corporation and the British European Airways Corporation. Almost at once, British Airways placed an order for five BAC/Aerospatiale Concorde supersonic airliners, continuing in the pioneering tradition of its predecessors. On 21 January 1976 a British Airways Concorde streaked into the sky towards Bahrain at twice the speed of sound on the world's first supersonic passenger service.

Little more than half a century had passed since that summer's day in 1919 when not so far away at Hounslow Heath, a canvas-clad DH16 biplane struggled into the air on its way to Paris at a sedate 124mph (200km/h).

Above:
A short-lived association with Cunard saw VC10s (and Boeing 707s) fly scheduled routes across the North Atlantic in joint titles.
BOAC

Below:
Heathrow in the early 1970s: BOAC's second Boeing 747 to be delivered marked the beginning of an exciting new era in the development of mass transportation of people.

British Airways Takes Over British Caledonian...

After months of public debate in the fall of 1987 the affirmative decision by the Monopolies and Mergers Commission towards the end of December, enabled British Airways to finally beat off the strong overseas competition from Scandinavian Airlines System (SAS) and take over its main UK competitor, British Caledonian. At £246 million the price was high, and there were several pre-conditions imposed by the Commission. Broadly these amounted to British Airways relinquishing within one month of the take-over all B.Cal's domestic route licences, together with unused rights between London/Gatwick and many destinations in central Europe. No further objections were to be lodged against applications by other carriers to compete on British Airways/British Caledonian routes which were not subject to Government agreements. In mitigation, British Airways was allowed to re-apply for all licences relinquished under these terms. Furthermore, British Airways offered to give up 5,000 slots at Gatwick and take over B.Cal's engineering and maintenance contracts with third party airlines.

The whole of the business of British Caledonian was transferred to British Airways on 14 April 1988 and full integration of the operations are now almost complete.

The B.Cal traditions and name – held in such high esteem by the air traveller – live on in the new charter company, **Caledonian Airways**, which absorbed **British Airtours** and the smaller charter element of **British Caledonian**. British Airways also initially acquired the 50% stake in **Cal-Air**, owned jointly with The Rank Organisation, but this was sold to Rank with effect from 24 May 1988.

The acquisition of British Caledonian has made British Airways Group an even more powerful force in world aviation, taking the airline a major step towards becoming Europe's first mega carrier. Together the combined airline carries over 23 million passengers a year to more than 165 destinations in 81 countries on all six continents with a fleet of over 200 aircraft. Coming into the aircraft park were two types new to British Airways: the Airbus A320 and the McDonnell Douglas DC-10-30. British Airways has never bought an Airbus, nor does it count itself among customers of the American manufacturer, McDonnell Douglas. Adding to this is some incompatibility of the engines, since B.Cal used General Electric powerplants for some of its 747s and DC-10-30s, whilst British Airways' widebodies are driven by Rolls-Royce and Pratt & Whitney turbofans.

Among the enormous benefits from the merger with B.Cal was the access to Gatwick's new and impressive North Terminal, opened on 18 March this year by Her Majesty The Queen. It offers Gatwick passengers an advanced standard of service initially accommodating 5 million a year, rising eventually to nine million passengers. The Terminal takes care of all intercontinental and some European services, while others will continue to operate from the existing South Terminal until the end of 1988. More services will be transferred from Heathrow to Gatwick in the near future.

The B.Cal check-in facilities of many years standing at Victoria station, recently transferred to the new £1 million Gatwick London Terminal in the Victoria Place complex above the station platforms, offers all Gatwick-bound passengers full city-centre check-in facilities.

It is confidently expected that B.Cal will earn British Airways a minimum of £400 million in extra revenue, boosting profits, though this must be set against the costs of acquisition and integrating the two airlines. This will take time and the full benefits may not become evident until the start of the next decade. Then, it will be full power ahead.

Coming into the aircraft park were two types new to British Airways: the Airbus A320 (*Below* **) and the McDonnell Douglas DC-10-30.**

2 British Airways Today – The World's Favourite Airline

Nothing concentrates the mind more wonderfully than, having made a commitment to an extravagant statement spawned by the fertile imagination of the advertising agency, being expected to live up to such high ideals. For British Airways, this has meant much greater effort over the past few years and the accolade, for such it has become, has been hard won and is richly deserved. Being the favourite is not in itself enough without also being the best and this is the ultimate goal British Airways has set itself with single-minded determination.

Today its activities and achievements are manifold and some facts and figures are clearly needed to illustrate the sheer size of the operation. Based at London Heathrow, the world's busiest international airport, the airline's principal business is the operation of international and domestic scheduled and charter air services for the carriage of passengers, cargo and mail. As the major international flag-carrier, British Airways is designated to exercise traffic rights held by the British Government under Air Services Agreements made with other countries. Necessary complementary services such as engineering (including airframe and engine overhaul), catering, telecommunications and data processing are provided not only for its own airline operations, but sold also to third parties. Operating revenue earned is now nearing a staggering £4 billion a year; an average of over £10 million per day.

British Airways has one of the most comprehensive international route networks of any airline, serving 165 cities in 81 countries on all six continents. This adds up to an unduplicated 430,000 miles (nearly 700,000km) of routes, equivalent to travelling more than 17 times around the world. In the last financial year, British Airways carried more than 20 million passengers on its scheduled services and another 3 million on charter flights, operated mainly by its subsidiary, British Airtours, now Caledonian Airways. In excess of one third of a million tonnes of cargo transported, also puts British Airways in the top ten of the air freight league.

All this has been made possible by a dedicated staff of some 43,000 men and women and a modern fleet of more than 200 aircraft. In a typical day, this fleet completes over 600 flight sectors in one part of the world or another and at the height of the travel season, almost 200 British Airways flights a day leave Heathrow alone for destinations near and far. Every two and a half minutes, somewhere, British Airways takes to the skies in a highly visible expression of its role as Britain's great airline.

Below:
Queen Elizabeth the Queen Mother celebrates 10 years of supersonic flight on board Concorde with British Airways' chairman Lord King.
British Airways/Adrian Meredith

The Magnificent Flying Machines

British Airways' modern fleet of aircraft is headed by the Anglo/French Concorde, the world's only supersonic airliner. Concorde is now well into its second decade of service with British Airways and has carried over one million passengers to date. Seven aircraft are used on scheduled services to New York, Washington, Miami and Barbados (on a seasonal basis), and on luxury supersonic charter flights which, in more ways than one, have become a booming business. Concorde also makes frequent 'guest' appearances at airshows and other special occasions all over the world where it invariably is the star attraction.

Flagship of the intercontinental fleet is the giant Boeing 747, more popularly known as the Jumbo Jet. The 40-strong fleet is made up of various models and include 16 early Pratt & Whitney-powered 747-100s, 18 747-200Bs with Rolls-Royce RB211 engines and six 747-200B Combis suitable for either passengers or freight, or a mixture of both. Most 747s have undergone a complete internal refurbishment and the advanced D4 modification of the RB211-524 power plant has been fitted to the Rolls-Royce-powered 747-200Bs. This latter £100 million programme has achieved substantial fuel economies and the greater range of the modified aircraft now allows nonstop opera-

Right:
Computers play an essential part in the efficient control of 101 functions within the airline. The control centre is located at Comet House.
British Airways/Adrian Meredith

Below:
One of the seven British Airways Concordes leading the way – supersonic style.
British Airways/Adrian Meredith

tions on a number of important routes to the Far East. From 1989 onwards, British Airways will place in service 19 Rolls-Royce-powered Boeing 747-400s. This latest version of the 747 family has a range of 8,000 miles (13,000km) and will consume about 18% less fuel. Eleven twin-engined 767-300s will also join the fleet from 1989 onwards.

Seventeen Lockheed TriStars fly to North and South America, Africa, the Gulf and parts of Asia, as well as operating scheduled services on high density European routes and holiday charters. A fleet of eight McDonnell Douglas DC10-30s operates services between Britain and the USA, Africa and the Gulf. The four types carry over 5 million passengers a year on intercontinental routes.

Equally impressive is the short/medium-haul fleet employed on domestic and European services, led by 32 Boeing 757 twin jets which are among the quietest and most fuel-efficient aircraft in service today. They have achieved great popularity vying in passenger appeal with the 45 Boeing 737s which have been the mainstay of the short-haul fleet since 1980. The recently-introduced 'state-of-the-art' Airbus A320 fleet will eventually number 10 aircraft.

In the Highlands and islands of Scotland, 12 HS 748 turboprops, soon to be supplemented by the larger ATP, provide a vital lifeline for the people in some of the remotest locations in the British Isles. Another British aircraft, the BAC One-Eleven, operates mainly out of the regional airports. All 39 aircraft have been completely refurbished, modernised and fitted with hushkits.

It is more than 20 years since the first fully-automatic landing by a Trident of BEA, and over 90% of the British Airways fleet is now fitted with Autoland. This allows blind landings to be made to the advanced CAT III standard, ie at zero decision height with forward visibility of only 250ft (75m). Only a small number of One-Elevens and 748s are not so fitted. The TriStar fleet can even operate to 'zero zero' standard when visibility is virtually non-existent.

Below:
Flight crew training without the use of simulators is unimaginable in today's high-technology age. The 757 simulator is among the most advanced in the world.
British Airways/Adrian Meredith

British Airways has also been in the forefront of the development of computerised flight systems which have now been installed in its Boeing 747 and 757 fleets. These are designed to guide the aircraft along the most fuel-efficient flight path.

Routes Across the World

British Airways' vast intercontinental route network ensures that its aircraft are seen from the Northern Isles in Scotland to Cape Town, and from Anchorage to Auckland. Starting at home, operations embrace extensive domestic services centred on Heathrow and Gatwick and reaching all parts of the United Kingdom and the Channel Islands. These routes, together with international flights operated out of Manchester, Birmingham and the main Scottish cities, carry six million passengers annually of which over half fly on the Super Shuttle routes from Heathrow to Glasgow, Edinburgh, Belfast and Manchester. In Europe, the British Airways route network is unrivalled, serving 60 destinations and including virtually every capital and major city in Eastern and Western Europe, Scandinavia and the Mediterranean countries. With many routes also from provincial airports, these add up to a frequent and comprehensive range of services for business and leisure traffic. As part of an agreement with the Allied Control Commission, British Airways also flies internal German services from Tegel Airport in West Berlin. This network, carrying over one million passengers a year, serves seven major German cities and the North Sea holiday island of Sylt. Across the North Atlantic, British Airways flies to 18 major cities spread across the United States, from the eastern seaboard to the West Coast and from Alaska in the north to sunny Florida. Cities served in Canada include Montreal, Toronto and Vancouver.

In South America, British Airways serves Venezuela, Brazil and Colombia and there are a number of Caribbean and mid-Atlantic island destinations including Antigua, Barbados, Bermuda, Jamaica, St Lucia, Trinidad and San Juan, Puerto Rico. On the African continent the British Airways presence is strong in countries in East, West, Central and Southern Africa. Many have close historic ties with the United Kingdom. British Airways is also the fastest way to fly to South Africa, serving Durban, Cape Town and Johannesburg. Principal holiday destinations are Kenya, Mauritius and the Seychelles.

Towards the East there is almost blanket coverage of the Gulf States and frequent services to India and Pakistan with a high amount of business traffic, but the leisure market is also particularly strong in Jordan and India. British Airways offers special services to this part of the world including customised tour programmes and a wider use of local languages by the cabin crews.

Beyond the Indian subcontinent, services stretch right across to the 'Land of the Rising Sun', taking in Bangladesh, Thailand, Malaysia, Singapore, South Korea, Philippines, China and Hong Kong and branching off to Australia and New Zealand.

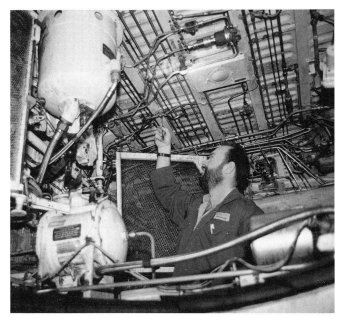

Above:
Visual inspection of a Boeing 737 hydraulic bay and components.
British Airtours

At Heathrow all intercontinental flights and the high density European services to Amsterdam and Paris are operated from the new Terminal 4, which was opened on 1 April 1986. All other Heathrow services use Terminal 1.

Gatwick's impressive new North Terminal, opened by Her Majesty The Queen on 18 March 1988, serves as the departure point for a range of international and some European services accounting for over 30 British Airways flights a day. In the new year, all remaining operations will be transferred from the South Terminal.

In Search of the Sun

The British Airways interests in the UK leisure market are served by **Caledonian Airways Ltd**, a wholly-owned subsidiary based at Gatwick Airport. A majority of flights serve the European and Mediterranean holiday centres, particularly in Spain, Portugal, Italy, Greece, Turkey and Yugoslavia, but there are also regular tour programmes and charters to destinations further afield. Most of the capacity is provided by Lockheed TriStars and Boeing 737s, with the main fleet bases located at Gatwick and Manchester. Caledonian Airways flies inclusive tours for most major tour operators including British Airways' own, trading under the brand names of Sovereign, Enterprise, Flair and Martin Rooks, which have recently been merged into a joint venture with Sunmed under the name of **Redwing,** creating the fourth largest in the UK market.

In addition to earnings from Caledonian Airways operations, a sizeable amount of revenue is also derived from the sale of British Airways whole-plane charters, including a considerable portion from Concorde. The number of passengers carried on charter flights per year is approximately three million which adds up to 13% of the airline's total passenger traffic. **Poundstretcher** is another

British Airways tour operating company which specialises in arrangements for the independent traveller, providing seats on British Airways services together with other facilities such as car hire and hotel accommodation. A similar service for traffic from the United States to Europe is offered by a US subsidiary company trading under the name of **Dollarstretcher.**

Cargo Business

British Airways is amongst the top 10 air cargo carriers in the world, earning the airline over £280 million a year. Exploiting to the full the enormous potential of its unparalleled worldwide route network, British Airways flies in excess of a third of a million tonnes of freight across the world in the holds of its passenger fleet, or on the massive cargo container decks of its Boeing 747 Combi passenger/freight aircraft, which can each carry up to 40 tonnes of cargo at the same time as 220 passengers. The Combis are in service on routes to Chicago, Hong Kong and to Tokyo. Since its inception in 1983, the Cargo Business Centre has gone from strength to strength culminating in 1986 with the completion of a multi-million pound expansion and modernisation programme of its air cargo facilities. This comprised a £7 million reconstruction of the Heathrow Cargocentre, the heart of its cargo network, a similar expenditure on a new up-to-date cargo terminal at Manchester International and another new centre at Birmingham Airport. British Airways' already substantial trucking network between the UK and continental points in support of its intercontinental flights, was further expanded and improved with a new distribution hub at Maastricht in the Netherlands which came into use in April 1986. Other trucking hubs have been opened at Helsingborg in southern Sweden and Lyon in France. A door-to-door service for shippers of small consignments of high value items is marketed under the name of **Speedbird Express**. This now covers most key areas of the British Airways route network. An **Express Handling Unit** ensures the highest standards of despatch, clearance and transhipment.

Engineering Excellence

A highly modern aircraft fleet needs a technical backup of matching sophistication. At Heathrow, British Airways operates one of the largest airline engineering bases in Europe, covering an area of 220 acres (89 hectares) and employing more than 6,000 engineering and maintenance staff. Another 1,500 engineering staff are employed at its Gatwick facilities. On any one typical day, some 25 aircraft pass through the hangars for attention which varies from routine servicing to a major overhaul, thus ensuring that the British Airways fleet is maintained to the highest possible standards. Apart from regular servicing requirements, there is a constant flow of additional modification programmes aimed at improving many aspects of safety, passenger comfort and economy.

British Airways also undertakes work for the Ministry of Defence, including engineering support for RAF TriStars engaged in South Atlantic operations and for a number of airlines. The total value to British Airways of engineering work for outside customers is now exceeding £70 million a year. The engines of most aircraft are taken to Treforest in South Wales, where **British Airways Engine Overhaul Ltd**, a wholly-owned subsidiary, operates one of the world's most up-to-date engine overhaul plants. Of all the highly skilled work undertaken there, only about half is for British Airways. The rest is for other customers around the world, bringing in a handsome £30 million each year. The 50-year-old Treforest factory is soon to be replaced by a new high technology plant at one of the company's existing sites at nearby Nantgarw.

Information Management

Computer and telecommunication systems in use within British Airways represent a staggering investment of £2.5 million a week in one of the largest and technically most advanced operations in the world today. Demands upon it continue to grow at some 40% per year and of a total of 1,300 staff, 600 alone are employed in the systems development department helping to ensure that British Airways retains its lead and keeps abreast of new developments in engineering, operations control and finance and material management. Typical of this are recent introductions of catering stock control, crew rostering and the installation of facilities to support its operations in the new Terminal 4, including a direct fibre optics link with the main Network Control Centre. Work is well advanced on a system to provide passengers with an inflight satellite telephone service for use over most of America, the North Atlantic, Europe and Africa. Also under consideration are hand-held video games, in-flight ticketing, seat-back videos and many other such innovations.

An air journey for most people begins long before take-off, usually with a telephone call to book a seat. This will be processed by the British Airways Business Systems, or BABS for short, which currently handles up to 60,000 bookings a day. With 12 main frame computers serving 20,000 British Airways computer terminals in 180 sales offices in 80 countries, as well as being linked to 23,000 travel agents around the world, BABS can prepare an itinerary, book seats, calculate the fare, reserve a rental car on arrival and even print the tickets. The departure control system computer at the airport can check in passengers, allocate seating and process special requirements such as wheelchairs, medical facilities, vegetarian diets and many more. Behind the scenes, computers also play an essential part in the efficient control of a hundred and one other functions in every department.

British Airways maintains a leading position in the development and provision of airline software and has already earned £11 million from the sale of computer consultancy, software packages and computer and tele-

Above.
Presiding over 80 qualified chefs is Willy Kraus, here providing plentiful and exotic evidence of British Airways catering.
British Airways/Adrian Meredith

communications services to other companies. More than 70 airlines feature on the list of customers and the latest contracts have been signed with such airline giants as United Airlines, Eastern Air Lines, Pan American and Japan Air Lines.

British Airways also has a 100% interest in Travel Automation Services Ltd which operates Travicom, a multiple-access travel agency reservations system, giving direct access into the computers of many other airlines, hotels and car rental companies. The airline has now joined forces with Covia, a subsidiary of UAL Corporation, parent company of United Airlines, as well as a number of European airlines, to develop Galileo, the next generation of computer reservation systems for the travel industry. Development cost is over £75 million and by 1990, Galileo is expected to be making the arrangements for 75 million journeys a year all over the world.

Human Resources

An Airline's Strength

The present and future challenges in the very competitive business of civil aviation demand a high standard of staff motivation and training, cutting right across the whole spectrum from basic skills to supervisory and management performance. Success is dependent on each employee, both individually and collectively as a team member and it is the principal role of the Human Resources department to ensure that the necessary skills are developed throughout the workforce to meet the airline's objective which is to be the best and most successful airline in the world.

British Airways constantly seeks to improve its customer service, both on the ground and in the air, and some 15,000 staff whose jobs bring them in direct contact with customers have attended professional training courses where the emphasis is, above everything else, on 'Putting People First'. Great strides have been made in the last few years towards that goal, as witnessed by a constant stream of industry awards and passenger accolades. Most of the airline's management training takes place at the training and conference centre at Chartridge in Buckinghamshire. British Airways are also leasing a recruitment selection and assessment centre at Meadowbank near Heathrow, to deal with the 200,000 job applications it receives each year.

Staff involvement in the airline's operations and objectives is also high on the list of priorities. A free weekly newspaper, *British Airways News*, is distributed to all staff and this is backed up with other specialist publications, video presentations on a wide range of subjects of interest and regular contacts between managers and employees. .

A training programme entitled 'To Be The Best' has been produced as a follow-up to the popular 'A Day in the Life' to help foster common awareness of factors affecting the airline's performance and staff are issued with an annual report incorporating the company's financial results. A profit-sharing scheme is in operation and a staff suggestion scheme known as 'Brainwaves', with individual rewards up to £10,000, has been going successfully since 1983.

Crew Recruitment and Training

Behind the outwardly smooth operation of every British Airways flight lies a continuous programme of training and in-service refresher courses. The flight crew training centre at Cranebank near Heathrow, is equipped with all 'state-of-the-art' facilities which include 11 advanced flight simulators for the Boeing 737, 747 and 757 jet aircraft, Lockheed TriStar, BAC One-Eleven and, of course, Concorde. Simulators for the McDonnell Douglas DC-10-30 and the new Airbus A320 are installed at the airline's Gatwick training centres. All of the airline's pilots – even the most experienced – are expected to attend regularly to rehearse in-flight procedures until they become second nature.

The latest 737 simulator is the first outside the United States to be fully certificated by the Federal Aviation Agency (FAA) for the training of American pilots, and several contracts have been negotiated with US airlines and aircraft manufacturers for its use during periods when it is not required for the training of British Airways crews. British Airways has earned £2.5 million from providing training facilities for other airlines and organisations. A fourth Boeing 747 flight simulator, part of a £9 million expansion programme of the airline's flight crew training facilities, was added in 1988. The new simulator represents the 747-200B Combi and has many advanced capabilities. Two for the new 747-400s are on order. Following the closure of the College of Air Training, British Airways has restarted an *ab initio* training programme which will run at least until the end of the century at the British Aerospace training school at Perth, sponsoring 150 cadets each year. A career guidance brochure is available to young men and women at school or university who wish to make their career in the air.

Cabin crew also need sound training for their demanding task. This is provided through meticulous classroom instruction using up-to-the-minute training aids including audio-visual techniques. Once they are qualified, they will join their colleagues who work aboard the British Airways fleet. A careful selection process ensures a good balance of youthful enthusiasm and mature experience, with only a slight current emphasis (55/45) in favour of the female sex.

An interesting innovation, some would say not before time, is a system whereby cabin crew managers up to senior level divide their time between their management duties on the ground and serving as active crew members in the air. This should go a long way towards maintaining a high standard of service and keeping management in close touch with the changing needs of today's discerning airline passenger.

The Way to a Passenger's Heart

A question most frequently asked of any airline and one on which answer many a judgement is based, is 'does it serve good food?'. In the case of British Airways, the answer has to be a definite yes. The British Airways catering team flies five million miles a year, researching and analysing worldwide food trends to enable 80 qualified chefs to create exciting new meals to meet the constantly changing palates of the traveller. The result is 460 different menus, co-ordinated through 140 catering stations and backed by a new computerised stock control system keeping track of the two million or so catering, items scattered around the globe. British Airways serves many local dishes on specific routes and, working closely with the Vegetarian Society, has an excellent selection of vegetarian meals to complement the wider range of special diets now offered. New menus are first served on Concorde and only those proving most popular are then gradually introduced into First, Club World and Economy Classes on other aircraft.

The accent is on wholesome and lighter meals, all served fresh or chilled, but never frozen. Serving tasty food on aircraft flying six miles high is by no means an easy task. Whilst everyone is aware that pressurisation offers a more comfortable flight, perhaps lesser known is the fact that it also reduces the perception of taste by anything up to 50%.

All intercontinental flights from Heathrow are catered for in the flight kitchen at Heathrow, newly enlarged and modernised at a cost of £8 million, and further improvements have been achieved with the completion of an extensive programme of in-flight catering facilities. This £40 million project involved the installation of new galleys in the Boeing 747s and an enhanced standardisation of catering equipment right across the fleet. Catering for the airline is a £100 million business, and 160,000 meals a week make British Airways the UK's top buyer of many food and drink items such as champagne (2,500 litres a week) and fresh and smoked salmon which weigh in at 25 tonnes a year.

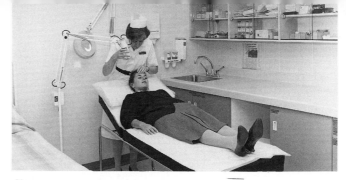

Above:
The British Airways Medical Service in action.
British Airways/Adrian Meredith

Travelling in Good Health

Looking after sick passengers is only one part of the work of the British Airways Medical Service, which ranges from the provision of passenger immunisation services, to dental care and investigating flight crew sleep patterns.

At Regent Street in London, British Airways operates an immunisation centre which has become established as one of the most eminent of its kind in Britain. Linked to the World Health Organisation in Geneva, it can offer the latest advice on health risks and conditions pertaining to every country in the world. Since being set up in 1982, the immunisation unit has dealt with some 200,000 customers. The opening of further centres is under consideration.

Unfortunately, not every flier enjoys good health at all times when embarking on a journey and it falls to the airline to ensure that the trip is made as comfortable as possible. British Airways, therefore, has set up a medical unit in Terminal 4 for passengers and staff, and a new unit is being developed at Heathrow's central area which will deal with stretcher cases and invalids from all four terminals. The airline carries over 10,000 known invalids per year, including hundreds of stretcher cases entering or leaving the United Kingdom.

British Airways Flying Club

Turning Fantasy into Reality

The British Airways Flying Club has provided recreational flying and training facilities since 1947, and boasts a membership of over 1,300 flyers from both within and without the airline staff. Located at Wycombe Air Park, near Marlow in Buckinghamshire, the flying club is operated by **Airways Aero Associations Ltd**, a wholly-owned subsidiary of **British Airways Associated Companies Ltd (BAAC)** which also has interests in Air Mauritius and GB Airways and in a number of hotels.

Highly professional instructors, among them many airline pilots who regularly fly international routes, turn that dream of piloting an aircraft into reality for many, providing instruction for approved PPL (Private Pilots' Licence) courses. There is no specific time limit to becoming a private pilot and in certain circumstances, depending on weather and skill, it can be achieved in as little as 38hrs. An average course, however, will more typically fall within the following timespan: first lessons up to circuit work (take-offs and landings) – 7hrs; dual circuits

– 5-10hrs; medical, aircraft and circuit test paper, solo consolidation, steep turns, forced landings practice, compass errors – 13hrs; instrument flying appreciation – 4hrs; cross-country flying – 10hrs; revision – 3hrs; and general flying test – 1hr. Additional lecture programmes are arranged within this period. Only five hours flying a year at regular intervals is required to keep the Pilots' Licence up to date.

Available advanced training includes Night, Instrument Meteorological Conditions (IMC), Flying Instructor, Radio Telephony and Twin and Commercial Pilots Type ratings. Aerobatic training can also be arranged. A modern fleet of aircraft consists of Piper single-engined types including the 2-seat Cherokee and Tomahawk. Inter-club rallies and competitions offer a chance to show off acquired skills and enjoy the company of fellow aviators. The club also has excellent social amenities at the airfield, including bar and restaurant – for after the flight.

The British Airways Look

A Touch of Class

The British Airways corporate identity is distinctive and sophisticated, incorporating the best of British style and heritage. It will keep the airline in the forefront of the international civil aviation industry well into the 1990s and presents a new public face more in line with recent changes, and the airline's aim of becoming the best in the world.

The new look was created by Landor Associates of America, one of the largest and most successful design houses, in consultation with the British company, Chester Jones. Landor brought to the job 40 years of experience in designing corporate identities for 150 clients, including 17 airlines. Work began in 1983 and it took the creative talents of 40 designers something like 18 months, to produce the complete package that was unveiled to the world in December 1984. Throughout that time close co-operation was maintained with the British Airways project team, which played an important part in refining the design to meet the airline's precise need. The brief given to the designers was to come up with a distinctive, modern identity which, through asserting the character of Britain's national airline, would also make British Airways stand out from all other airlines. The design was to reflect its customer orientation in terms of colour and warmth, it was to be professional and precise, and last but not least, was to be suitable for all the thousands of items that bear the

British Airways' name. This was of particular importance as, for the first time in its history, British Airways attempted to achieve a total visual identity which extends to every facet of its operation, including the exterior and interior of aircraft, sales shops, lounges, vehicles, tickets, stationery and more. The reactions to a number of proposals were tested within the airline and in several countries around the world, and the design was eventually firmed up around three colours: pearl grey, rich midnight blue and Speedwing red. The Speedbird, in use since the days of Imperial Airways, was the inspiration behind the dramatic red Speedwing, which provides an essential link between the nose and the fin of the aircraft and forms a close relationship with the stylised Union Jack. The Speedwing is the symbol that is seen everywhere and on everything and, together with the coat of arms, forms the principal elements of the design. The British Airways name is styled in capital letters using a bold Optima typeface.

Flying Envoys

The outstanding bearers of the British Airways image are, of course, its fleet of 200 aircraft which, more than anything else, will ensure a constant presence at airports around the world. The tailfin, the most easily recognisable feature, is divided into two halves, with the upper in midnight blue promoting the coat of arms in grey above a quartered Union Jack, set into the lower pearl grey. The British Airways titles are traditionally placed and aligned with the red Speedwing, which runs almost the full length of the fuselage, providing a bold separation between the pearl grey top and midnight blue lower fuselage and engine nacelles. Aircraft registrations and names are highlighted in grey against the blue. Slight variations exist within the Concorde fleet. Concorde has an equally distinctive all-white fuselage in order to reflect the heat and keep to a minimum the extremely high surface temperatures generated in supersonic flight.

The Caledonian Airways fleet combines the best of both British Airways and British Caledonian. The fuselage features the pearl grey upper and midnight blue under-side of the former, with the red speedwing replaced by a narrow gold cheatline. The tailfin displays the familiar 'Lion Rampant' of B.Cal in the standard blue and gold arrangement. The word Caledonian is reproduced on the cabin roof in the same typeface as British Airways.

Repainting the entire British Airways fleet has been a massive task, which has taken nearly three years to complete. It takes almost 220galls of paint (or about 1,000 l) and a 14-man team 18 days, working a seven-day double shift, to transform a Boeing 747. With a limited paint life, it all has to be repeated again in five years' time.

No sooner was the airline nearing the end of this work, it had to initiate a new re-painting programme involving the entire British Caledonian fleet and that of British Airtours. Some of the latter had to be re-painted in the new Caledonian Airways livery. Extensive interior refitting to bring the aircraft up to British Airways standard was also part of this exercise.

The Badge of Honour

The coat of arms, which today adorns everything from baggage tags to aircraft, adding a sense of grace and tradition, was granted to British Airways in January 1975, in recognition of its service to the nation. Prepared by York Herald of Arms, Dr Conrad Swan, it was inspired in part by the Union Jack which, although not an official national flag, is recognised all over the world as representative of Great Britain and everything British. The shield is sup-ported appropriately by Pegasus, the winged horse, and a lion guardant winged at the shoulders. Above the shield is the helm and crest, consisting of a sunburst, symbolic of energy, strength and vitality, rising from an astral crown. The motto is 'To Fly to Serve'.

The British Airways coat of arms

Fitting out the Thousands

A new look for the staff to match the new look airline was part and parcel of the transformation. After months of exhaustive research and consultations with thousands of British Airways staff, British fashion designer Roland Klein produced a completely new housestyle for staff in every-day contact with customers. Similar attention was given to the workwear designs by John Playfair of the House of André Peters. About 16,000 men and women – some 40% of the workforce – wear the Klein uniforms and another 15,000 the protective clothing of André Peters. Between the two groups, this adds up to 600,000 items of uniforms and accessories. Caledonian Airways stewardesses wear the well-known tartan uniform which had been a symbol of warm and attentive service throughout the history of British Caledonian.

Everything in life subtly changes and dates, and airline liveries are no exception. Although the change set British Airways back by several million pounds and took three years to complete, it has clearly been a worthwhile investment and will help British Airways to maintain a strong profile in the marketplace for years to come.

3 British Airways – Ambassador to the World

It was back more than half a century ago in the days of Imperial Airways that Britain began opening up the world with its Empire routes to India, Australia and South Africa. These still form some of the main arteries of the British Airways route network but the North Atlantic routes, among the last great distances to be conquered by air, have outstripped all others in significance and now provide British Airways with some 30% of its operating revenue.

A total of 18 gateway cities are served in the United States from which frequent connections are available by other carriers to literally hundreds of US destinations. The cities are New York, Boston, Washington, Philadelphia and Pittsburgh in the east; Detroit and Chicago in the mid-west; Los Angeles, San Francisco, San Diego and Seattle on the west coast; Anchorage, Alaska in the far north; and Atlanta, Houston, Dallas/Ft. Worth, Orlando, Tampa and Miami in the south. During the height of the summer season British Airways offers daily wide-body flights to and from most of these gateways, and no less than six flights a day between London and New York, including two supersonic services. There are also direct daily services between New York and Manchester. Aircraft used across the Atlantic are the Boeing 747, DC-10, Lockheed TriStar and Concorde. First, Club World and Economy classes are available on each subsonic service, while a one-class deluxe service is offered on Concorde.

Number one destination in the USA is, of course, New York, followed in order of importance and popularity by Los Angeles, Chicago, Boston and Miami. The growth market at the present time is Florida, with Orlando and Tampa doing particularly well and Miami maintaining its place as the main terminal for onward connections to Central and South America.

Chicago is one of British Airways' largest American hubs, where its daily service connects with the United Airlines system, giving extensive coverage of the USA as far west as Hawaii. At Pittsburgh, flights link into the USAir network of more than 70 cities, mainly in the industrial heartland and the Ohio Valley. At Los Angeles and San Francisco British Airways flights are scheduled to connect with Delta Air Lines. All offer special fare packages for passengers wanting to visit several cities on their networks. Close co-operation exists between British Airways and United Airlines, the US domestic giant, following the establishment in December 1987 of a worldwide marketing partnership giving British Airways additional strength in the United States domestic market. Customer advantages include convenient connecting flights to United's 160 cities network, through one-stop check-in, and the joint sale of package holidays in Europe and America. Other benefits are joint advertising, enhancement of the two airlines' reservation systems – BABS and Apollo – and co-ordination of flight schedules at British Airways' 18 gateways.

In Canada, British Airways flies daily to Montreal and Toronto, and four times a week to Vancouver, British Columbia, using 747s and TriStars. Convenient connections on local airlines are scheduled to Ottawa, Winnipeg, Calgary and Victoria. 'Ministays Stopover' packages are available at all three British Airways destinations.

British Airways currently carries a total of more than two million passengers annually across the North Atlantic at an average load factor of 65-70%. Cargo business continues to record steady growth and some 50,000 tonnes of freight are transported annually between the USA and Britain in each direction. Commodities range from automotive and

Right:
British Airways' Terminal 4 on the south side of Heathrow Airport, opened in April 1986.
British Airways/Adrian Meredith

heavy machinery parts from Chicago and Detroit to flowers, fresh fruit and vegetables from sunny California and Florida.

Nerve centre of the North American operation is the new British Airways suburban headquarters in the Bulova Center at Jackson Heights, Queens, close to La Guardia Airport. The new 145,000sq ft (13,445sq m) of office space which replaced the smaller and significantly more expensive facilities on Park Avenue in the heart of New York City, provides a modern working environment all on one floor for 700 of the 1,300 staff nationwide, housing the main reservations centre together with management and sales personnel, while still leaving room for expansion. A smaller, supplementary reservations facility is presently being maintained at Chicago, but this will eventually be absorbed into New York.

A Unique Airline

British Airways Terminal at JFK

Uniquely among foreign flag-carriers, British Airways is the only airline to have its own terminal building at New York's J.F. Kennedy International Airport. It is also the only airport terminal owned by British Airways. Construction work on the 330,000sq ft (30,600sq m) building, designed specifically to accommodate 747s and Concorde, began on the 26-acre (10.5 hectare) site in January 1967 and was completed three years later. Following an extensive $25 million renovation scheme carried out between 1983 and 1986, the terminal was rededicated by Princess Alexandra in June 1986. With the inauguration of the new Terminal 4 at Heathrow Airport a few months previously, and Gatwick Airport's North Terminal in March 1988, transatlantic passengers now have modern terminal facilities at both ends, offering a greatly improved service. Since the original opening in 1970, more than 30 million passengers have utilised the terminal and there have been 200,000 aircraft movements.

The exterior architectural character of the building has been shaped by sloping glass walls and white honeycomb fascia panels incorporating the British Airways corporate image, topped by a high trussed steel roof spanning 200ft (60m) between concrete cores and cantilevering 60ft (18m) on all sides. The colour scheme is continued

through to the main concourse and elsewhere in the interior.

The upper departure level incorporates a travel centre, buffet restaurant, English theme cocktail lounges and newspaper, gift and duty-free shops. On the Mezzanine can be found the Speedwing Lounge and Executive Club, both with direct access to the departure gate areas. The exclusive Concorde Lounge is situated at Gate 5 where it affords a splendid view of the supersonic aircraft. A bar, appropriately named 'New York New York', is located on the lower arrivals level outside Customs and Immigration. A main feature of the terminal facilities are the inter-level, ramp loading bridges, known as 'luffing-bridges', which provide covered, all-weather access between aircraft and building. These projecting bridges move up and down on the face of the building to serve both departure and arrival levels, obviating the need for passengers to use stairs. A new system of baggage handling using larger belts – devised in part by British Airways employees – facilitates quick and efficient baggage movement and minimises damage to luggage.

The British Airways terminal is also home from home for a number of other airlines, providing regular employment

Above:
The TriStar cockpit is sophisticated, being fitted with a computerised flight management system.
British Airways/Adrian Meredith

Above:
The British Airways Travel Shop in the Strand, London, was the first to be redesigned in the new corporate image. This will be progressively applied to shops worldwide.
British Airways/Adrian Meredith

for 1,000 people. Among them are USAir, Eastern and Tower Air, all of the United States, together with Air Jamaica, BWIA, Air Portugal, SAA and LTU. United Airlines will share the Terminal from 1990.

In-flight Telephones and Television
For the first time ever, passengers will be able to make phone calls across the Atlantic and over the African continent. A telephone service from the air has only previously been available on US domestic flights using ground-to-air communications. British Airways, setting the pace in both customer service and technological advance, has joined with British Telecom International and Racal

Decca Advanced Development to conduct exclusive trials on three Boeing 747s. This has been made possible by a decision of the International Maritime Satellite Organisation to free spare satellite capacity for aeronautical communications. Telephones are fitted to the aircraft bulkhead and calls can be made via a ground-based telephone operator in the United Kingdom. A dedicated satellite antenna at Goonhilly Downs in Cornwall serves as an earth station solely for aeronautical use. At the present time passengers are only able to make outgoing calls, but British Airways hopes ultimately to offer a two-way service. In the longer term, satellite communication is expected to provide direct links between the aircraft flightdeck and the airline's ground-based computers, to enable more effective monitoring of flight performance and fuel efficiency. Skyvision, British Airways' new 'TV station in the sky', is shown on flights of over three hours duration. Programmes from broadcasting companies around the world include sport, travel, light entertainment and children's shows. The inflight TV system has been created for British Airways by Spafax Airline Network.

Long-haul

Serving the Caribbean and South America
British Airways flies direct to more destinations in the Caribbean than any other international airline. Points served include Antigua, Barbados, Bermuda, Jamaica (both Kingston and Montego Bay in conjunction with Air Jamaica), St Lucia, the Bahamas and Trinidad and Tobago. The airline also offers a choice of flights to Barbados and St Lucia from both London Heathrow and Gatwick Airports. Virtually all the smaller Caribbean islands within the Leeward, Windward and Virgin groups, such as Anguilla, Dominica, Grenada, St Kitts, Nevis, St Maarten, St Thomas,

St Vincent and Tortola, are within easy reach via the LIAT (Leeward Islands Air Transport) network.

Following the much publicised route swap with British Caledonian in 1985, British Airways once again took on responsibility for the flag services to South America and presently serves four destinations on the continent. The nonstop flight to Rio de Janeiro is the fastest service on this prestigious route. It leaves London every Saturday and Thursday, arriving at Rio's Galeao International Airport 10 hours later and both flights continue on to São Paulo, Brazil's still fast-growing commercial centre. A similar frequency is also offered to the Venezuelan capital of Caracas, via Port of Spain, Trinidad. Traditionally supporting mostly oil-related business, a slowly-awakening appreciation of the tourism potential in this still unspoilt country is beginning to attract the leisure traffic. One of the two flights to Caracas carries on to Bogota, providing the only direct link between the UK and Colombia.

Above:
The present Boeing 747 fleet is made up of three different models, totalling 40 aircraft. Nineteen more of the longer range 747-400 series will be added from 1989 onwards.
British Airways/Adrian Meredith

Convenient onward flights are available by local airlines to Quito, Lima, La Paz, Santiago, Asunçion, Montevideo and Buenos Aires. The once profitable British Airways service to Buenos Aires and beyond fell victim to the Falklands conflict in 1982 and is destined to remain dormant until such time as full diplomatic relations with Argentina are resumed. Within the limitations imposed by this artificial situation, British Airways is, however, working behind the scenes towards a reactivation of this service.

All South American destinations are served by Boeing 747s seating up to 376 passengers.

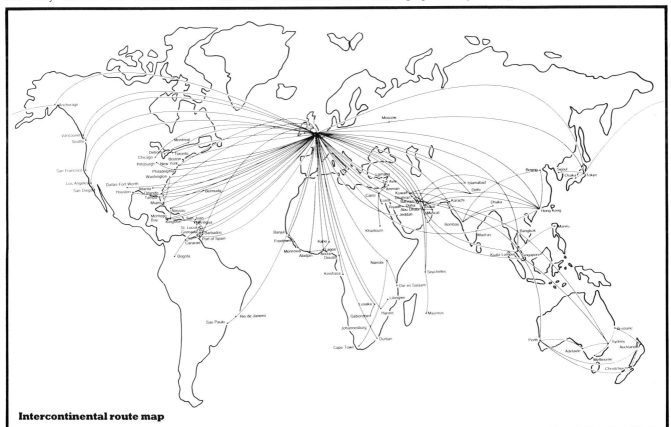

Intercontinental route map

Bridging the Gulf

Prolific business activities and close historical ties between Britain and the Arab world are the main reasons why British Airways flies to more points in the Middle East, more often, than any other airline. The accent is most definitely on business and all 747, DC-10 and TriStar services offer the choice of First Class sleeperseats, Club World and Economy with free bar and inflight entertainment in all classes. Seating in Club World is only six-abreast, in three pairs, on the main deck of the TriStar (seven-abreast in the DC-10 and 747) and four-abreast on the 747 upper deck.

Arabic cabin staff are present on all flights and other extensions of the airline's customer services include tour programmes for those passengers wanting to see the sights, especially in Jordan, and the Middle East Visitors Service (MEVS) to assist Arab passengers arriving and departing from London Heathrow Airport. A MEVS welcome desk and office are situated in Terminal 4 especially to help those visitors who speak little or no English. All MEVS staff are fluent in Arabic and are there to meet and escort travellers through all formalities and assist with hotel bookings and suchlike. A MEVS limousine is also available for hire. Another plus for the businessman is a late check-out facility at all Middle Eastern Sheraton hotels to take account of late evening departures from the Gulf to the Far East and Australasia.

British Airways services link London daily with Kuwait and Bahrain, nine times a week with Dubai (United Arab Emirates); six times a week with Abu Dhabi (UAE) and Muscat in the Sultanate of Oman; once with Doha, Qatar and three times with Amman, Jordan.

The major Saudi Arabian cities of Dhahran, Jeddah and Riyadh are served eight times, four times and twice a week respectively.

India and Beyond

Reaching the Indian subcontinent was the first major achievement in establishing the Empire links in the days of Imperial Airways. In nearly 60 years which have passed since, the route has lost little in importance and none of the mystique attached to this fascinating part of the world. Today British Airways flies up to eight times a week from London to India serving Bombay, Delhi and Madras, its Boeing 747s completing the nonstop journey in just eight hours. Since the winter of 1986, Bombay and Delhi have also been served from Manchester. Frequent connecting flights to Calcutta, India's largest conurbation some 900 miles (1,500km) to the east, are available via Indian Airlines. Business and ethnic traffic make up the largest proportion of the 200,000 passengers carried annually, but tourism supports a fair share of this total. For the First Class and Club World passenger travelling to and from India, British Airways has initiated its exclusive 'Gateway India' service, designed to ease the way through all the formalities involved when passing through Bombay and Delhi airports. On arrival, the passenger is met and given assistance with immigration formalities, or provided with an escort service in a special air-conditioned bus if transferring to another flight. When leaving India a similar standard of service applies.

On the same landmass lie Pakistan to the west, and Bangladesh to the east. Both are served by British Airways, twice or three times a week, routeing via a number of Gulf destinations. Destinations are the Pakistan capital of Islamabad, Karachi, the country's principal port and commercial centre, as well as Dhaka, capital of Bangladesh. All flights are operated by 747s.

Beyond the Indian subcontinent, British Airways services reach out daily to Bangkok in Thailand, Singapore, and the Crown colony of Hong Kong, due to revert to Chinese ownership in 1997. Tokyo, the capital of Japan – 'Land of the Rising Sun' – is also served up to twice daily. Three of these flights a week are extended to Osaka which, together with Tokyo and Nagoya, are all in close proximity and account for one-third of Japan's population and two-thirds of its entire industrial production. Other Far East destinations, served at lesser frequencies, are Kuala Lumpur in Malaysia, Seoul, venue of the 1988 Olympic Games in South Korea, Manila in the Philippines and Beijing (formerly Peking), capital of the People's Republic of China.

The Longest Way

Today's routes to Australia are a far cry from the 'Empire' link of 50 years ago which took all of 12 days and several changes of aircraft, not to mention the two train journeys en route. What must then have seemed an interminable distance is now covered by British Airways' long range Boeing 747s in under 22hrs, depending on the routeing, carrying up to 376 passengers in restful surroundings and comfort.

The link with Australia is still among Britain's most important routes with 10 flights a week in each direction, transporting a quarter of a million passengers a year. Five state capitals are served from a minimum of two flights a week up to a daily frequency. The cities are Adelaide (South Australia), Brisbane (Queensland), Melbourne (Victoria), Perth (Western Australia) and Sydney (New South Wales). Flights are routed in a variety of ways, taking in either Abu Dhabi, Bahrain and Singapore, or with a single stopover at Bangkok. Two services are extended across the Tasman Sea to Auckland, New Zealand. Christchurch, the principal city of New Zealand's South Island, is also served, the flight leaving Heathrow on Wednesday. All flights are through-plane services, saving the inconvenience of having to change aircraft along the way.

British Airways offers a variety of fares to enable visitors to see more of the continent. These include low-cost Saver fares, permitting one stopover in each direction in such favoured tourist spots as Singapore, Bangkok or Hong Kong, as well as a 'Circle Australia' fare which, for a small additional charge, allows the traveller to visit as many as five Australian cities. Special internal fares are available in conjunction with Ansett Airlines. Stopovers at Perth, Brisbane or Sydney are possible when visiting New Zealand on a Saver fare. British Airways also offers a choice of three 'Round-the-World' fares in co-operation with Qantas, United Airlines and Air New Zealand, which include Australia in their itineraries. The journey can be broken an unlimited number of times and there is also an option to include a flight on Concorde across the Atlantic.

African Arrows

More than half a century ago Britain's flag services to Africa were carved out of the continent in a titanic pioneering effort by Imperial Airways. Handed over to British Airways via BOAC, they remain among the airline's key long-haul routes, with those to the Republic of South Africa the principal revenue earners. British Airways flies daily to Johannesburg, the largest city, with a nonstop service every Monday, Tuesday and Friday. On other days, flights operate via Nairobi. The Jumbo to Cape Town is equally popular with both business and leisure travellers, and British Airways is also the fastest way to fly to Durban, the coastal capital of Natal. The midweek night service takes less than 13hrs and that is still almost two hours faster than by any other airline. All South African services are flown by the Boeing 747, laid out in three-class configuration with sleeper seats in the First Class cabin. 'Fly and Stay' packages combining flight with accommodation in selected luxury hotels at all three destinations, together with convenient connecting flights from UK regional airports and through check-in for both domestic and intercontinental sectors, make British Airways a favourite carrier to the southern hemisphere.

Lockheed TriStar wide-body jets are used on four weekly services to Cairo, Egypt. Two of these fly on to Khartoum in neighbouring Sudan, with a week-end service to Luxor. All these destinations are steeped in air transport history, as are Nairobi, British Airways' most important East African port of call with daily nonstop flights; Lilongwe, Malawi; Harare, Zimbabwe and Dar-es-Salaam, the capital of Tanzania.

Of much more recent history are the once-a-week 747 flights to the exotic holiday islands of Mauritius and the Seychelles in the Indian Ocean off East Africa, flown via Bahrain or Nairobi, and the direct short-haul flights to Marrakech and Casablanca in Morocco, inaugurated on 4 May 1986.

Britain's important flag services to West Africa and those to Zaire, Zambia and Botswana in central and southern Africa, were formerly operated by British Caledonian Airways. These now serve Banjul in The Gambia; Freetown, Sierra Leone; Monrovia, Liberia; Abidjan, Ivory Coast; Accra, Ghana; Kano and Lagos, Nigeria; Douala, Cameroon; Kinshasa, Zaire; Lusaka, Zambia and Gaborone, Botswana. With the exception of the Nigerian city of Lagos which has daily flights, all other destinations are served once or twice a week with DC-10-30s, departing from Gatwick's North Terminal.

The Young Flyers Airline

British Airways counts a large number of young people among its passengers and offers a range of services and attractive facilities to make their flight more enjoyable. The airline also recognises the fact that the young person of today could well be the business traveller of tomorrow.

All young flyers under the age of 12 travelling alone are looked after by British Airways from the moment they check-in, until they are handed over to their parent or guardian at the other end of their journey. During busy school holiday periods, specially trained escorts help the young flyer with departure and arrival procedures at Heathrow, and on flights where there are a group of children travelling alone, an inflight escort will accompany them on board the aircraft. All escorts are experienced members of staff who have undergone a thorough training course and have special knowledge of children's requirements. All this is supplied free of charge, but an onboard escort service for an individual travelling alone can be provided on a fee-paying basis.

At peak periods there is a special check-in area and lounge set aside in Heathrow's Terminal 4 and Gatwick's new North Terminal for young flyers departing on intercontinental flights, with similar facilities available in Terminal 1 for short-haul sectors.

In-flight entertainments for children include their own audio channel and an activity/games pack to avoid the boredom of a long journey. British Airways also tries to arrange visits to the flightdeck whenever possible.

Terminal 4

Terminal 4, owned and operated by the British Airports Authority (BAA), has been built to meet the continued growth in air travel, increasing Heathrow Airport's capacity by eight million to a total of 38 million passengers a year and is capable of handling 2,000 passengers an hour in both directions.

Planning of the new terminal started in 1973, and after a public enquiry and lengthy government deliberations the go-ahead was given in December 1979. There followed 18 months of consultations with the local authorities on major environmental issues before work began in June 1981. At peak periods, construction work on the huge £200 million project involved up to 1,000 workers with expenditure levels reaching £1 million a week. The official opening ceremony on 1 April 1986 was performed by their Royal Highnesses The Prince and Princess of Wales.

From the outset, Terminal 4 was designed around space, speed, simplicity, service and safety, incorporating lessons learnt from studying other passenger terminals around the world. It is the first terminal building in Britain to completely segregate arriving and departing passenger flows on different floors. The entire route from the aircraft to the terminal exits, and vice versa, remains on one level, with no lifts, stairs or escalators complicating the movement of passengers, baggage trolleys or wheelchairs. The building is 2,135ft (650m) long by 82ft (25m) wide with an open plan concourse containing 72 check-in desks in a single line with space for eight more. There are 17 aircraft stands accessible immediately from the concourse, all large enough to accommodate every widebody jet for the present and the foreseeable future. The new terminal has its own underground station and road access from the M3, M4 and M25 motorways. Links with Terminals 1, 2 and 3 in the central area are provided by means of a new road connection with the cargo tunnel.

Operation Overnight

To state that the terminal has been taken over by British Airways is no exaggeration, for on the night of 11/12 April 1986 all intercontinental flights and the short-haul services to Paris and Amsterdam were transferred to Terminal 4 in what was the biggest-ever operational move in the history of the airline. Between the last scheduled evening flight and the arrival of the next morning's first service, British Airways had barely eight hours to move lock, stock and barrel from the central area to Terminal 4. The massive exercise required months of precise planning including full-scale rehearsals and entailed shifting the place of work of 2,200 staff and equipment including almost 1,000 vehicles. Most vehicles had to be towed from Terminal 3, and throughout the night a seemingly endless convoy of tractors, cargo dollies, elevator trucks and others, led by the British Airways Pipe Band, snaked its way across the otherwise deserted runways. With the dawn arrived BA144 from Dhaka. The dummy runs were over and Terminal 4 was ready to take on the world.

Easy Comings and Goings

Terminal 4 has been designed to make things simple and easy for British Airways passengers from the moment of alighting by car, taxi, bus or underground, to boarding the aircraft. The terminal building has four entrances to the departures area, which are clearly signposted and numbered for easy reference. Doors 1 and 2 lead to British Airways long-haul and Economy and Group check-in; Door 3 to British Airways Paris and Amsterdam services,

as well as to KLM, NLM and Air Malta flights, and Door 4 is for British Airways Club, First Class and Concorde passengers.

Once inside the departures hall, British Airways passengers have a choice of 64 check-in desks each equipped with the latest computer technology, and for the first time a low-level check-in desk has been provided for travellers in wheelchairs. Passengers enter passport control and security check through a central channel before emerging into the all-in-one airside lounge, replacing the conventional system of individual lounges and final gaterooms. Facing the passenger are four British Airways customer service and information desks and there are areas set aside for Young Flyers and 'special care' passengers. Moving walkways transport passengers effortlessly to their boarding points. Gently sloping boarding jetties allow disabled passengers to be taken right to the door of the aircraft in their own wheelchairs.

British Airways has three special lounges for key categories of passengers, situated just off the departure concourse. These are the Speedwing Lounge for Concorde and First Class passengers with direct access to the aircraft; the Executive Club Lounge and the Oasis Lounge for transfer passengers. All have superb facilities including bar, refreshments, television, telephones, newspapers and magazines; transfer passengers with long connecting times can avail themselves additionally of changing rooms, showers and sleeper-style seats.

Inbound passengers disembark on the lower level and proceed to the immigration area, again via moving walkways. After passport control, there is a small buffer lounge with television monitors indicating the number of the baggage carousel allocated to the flight. In the baggage hall are Customer Service and Lost and Found Desks to deal with any passenger problems. After passing through customs, passengers have at their disposal British Airways domestic check-in and transfer and sales and reservations facilities, together with the full range of the usual car hire, hotel and onward travel services. An inter-terminal bus service for transfer passengers departs at five-minute intervals.

With over 40 services a day and 4.5 million passengers a year, Terminal 4 is, without doubt, the major British Airways gateway to the world.

Cross-section of passenger flow in Terminal 4

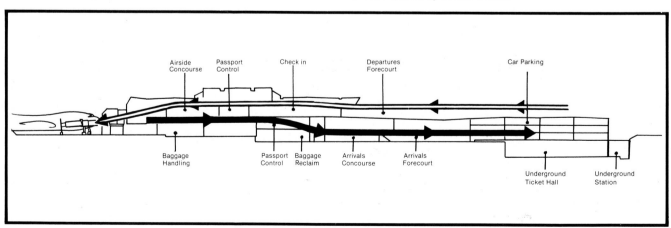

Above:
BEA operated a fleet of 39 turboprop Vickers Viscount 800s which helped to keep it in the forefront of domestic and European operations during the 1960s.
Anthony Wirkus

 British Airways Concorde – The Ultimate Flying Experience

Since entering service on 26 January 1976, the British Airways Concorde fleet has made some 20,000 supersonic flights totalling over 65,000 flying hours. In that time it has carried more than one million passengers over a distance of 60 million miles and with a perfect safety record. The Concorde story began 20 years before the first commercial service when independent design studies into supersonic transport were initiated simultaneously by Bristol Aircraft Co in the UK and Sud-Aviation (later to become Aerospatiale) in France. Financial considerations and the fact that, technically, work was proceeding along very similar lines, led to a pooling of resources and in 1962, agreement was reached between the British Aircraft Corporation (formed by the merger of Bristol, English Electric and Vickers), Sud-Aviation, Rolls-Royce and SNECMA, the French engine manufacturer, for the joint development of a supersonic airliner, appropriately named Concorde.

This was the first major collaborative venture in Europe and all design, development and construction work was shared between these participants. The end product was a 120-seat delta-wing aircraft powered by four Rolls-Royce/SNECMA Olympus 593 turbojets and capable of flying at more than twice the speed of sound. One prototype and one pre-production aircraft was built in each country and prototype 001 made its maiden flight at Toulouse on 2 March 1969, followed by the British 002 at Filton on 9 April. Five thousand hours of testing went into Concorde, making it the most tested aircraft in aviation history. It remains to this day the only supersonic airliner certificated for passenger transport.

In spite of the enormous development costs of £1.5 billion, the future for Concorde was beginning to look assured with 74 aircraft ordered or optioned by some of the world's major airlines. British Airways was to become the first supersonic airline when it placed an order for five

aircraft announced in July 1972, and Air France followed suit soon after with an order for four aircraft. Storm clouds, however, were quickly gathering and rapidly escalating costs of aircraft and fuel, together with a vociferous and powerful environmental lobby, quickly reduced the order book to these nine aircraft. Production eventually ceased after the completion of 16 aircraft.

Today, both British Airways and Air France have seven aircraft, two production aircraft remain at Filton and Toulouse and the prototypes and pre-production models

Below:
Concorde comes into the hangar much more often than the subsonic types in the fleet. Its first Service check takes place after only 100hrs and involves 10 men working 24hrs.
British Airways/Adrian Meredith

are preserved as museum pieces at Yeovilton, Duxford, Le Bourget and Orly.

The critics have long been silenced and what was once derided in some quarters as a big white elephant has, in British Airways service especially, been transformed into a sleek white bird flying successfully across the Atlantic, representing a standard of speed and in-flight luxury unsurpassed in today's era of mass travel. It remains a symbol of tremendous human ingenuity and technological achievement.

The Aircraft

Concorde is of low-wing cantilever configuration with a large area delta wing and a long, narrow fuselage with a maximum internal width of 8ft 7in (2.62m). Overall length is 204ft (62m) and the wing span measures 83ft 9in (25.5m).

Power is provided by four specially designed Rolls-Royce/SNECMA Olympus 593 mark 610 turbojet engines in underwing nacelles, each capable of developing a thrust of 38,050lb (169kN) inclusive of 20% reheat. Reheat adds fuel to the final stage of the engine to produce the extra power necessary for take-off and the transition to supersonic flight. Fuel capacity is 26,342 imp galls (119,250l), most of which is held in the wing. Apart from fuelling the engines, the large volume of fuel acts as a heat sink to reduce wing temperatures during prolonged supersonic flight.

Take-off speed is 217kt (300km/h), some 30% above that of subsonic jets and landing speeds are also correspondingly higher. The steep angle of attack at low subsonic speed due to its delta platform, necessitates a lowering of the characteristic 'droop nose', to improve the pilot's visibility of the ground during take-off, initial climb, approach and landing. Field length requirements at maximum weights are 11,250ft (3,425m) for take-off and 7,200ft (2,200m) for landing. Range with full payload and fuel reserves is 4,050 miles (6,500km). Maximum possible passenger capacity is 144, but in British Airways service Concorde carries a much more comfortable complement of 100 passengers.

Normal cruising speed is Mach 2 (average 1,350mph or 2,175km/h) at altitudes up to its service ceiling of 60,000ft (18,250m) and this speed can be maintained for up to three hours. In most other respects, Concorde behaves much as a subsonic aircraft.

The Supersonic Schedules

The prime British Airways Concorde route is London-New York, flown twice daily in both directions. The morning flight leaves Heathrow's Terminal 4 at 1030hrs and Concorde's ability to cruise at twice the speed of sound combined with the five-hour time difference, means that the traveller arrives in New York at the start of business that same day, fresh enough for the working day ahead. With an average flying time of only 3hrs and 25min, the 3,660 miles (5,900km) transatlantic crossing is reduced to a pleasant medium-haul journey. The evening flight is scheduled to leave London at 1900hrs, arriving at J.F. Kennedy Airport in the late afternoon.

Eastbound, the morning departure gets the traveller to London in time for dinner and the early afternoon service arrives later that same evening. It is, of course, possible to fly the Concorde 'Cannonball' – there and back in one day. The 0920hrs touchdown in New York allows businessmen almost four hours for an important meeting by using either the conference facilities adjacent to the Concorde Lounge at the airport or; alternatively, the fast helicopter link for a meeting in the city centre.

This complimentary helicopter service, operated by **New York Helicopters (HD)**, is available to Concorde passengers between Kennedy, La Guardia and Newark Airports (for onward connections only), as well as to the East 34th Street Heliport or the World Trade Center in downtown Manhattan. Arriving passengers are met by New York Helicopters staff at the British Airways information desk in the customs hall and transferred by minibus the short distance to the helicopter at TWA's international terminal. The flight to Manhattan in the Sikorsky S-58 takes no more than 10min.

Washington DC is served nonstop three times a week, leaving London at 1300hrs on Tuesdays, Thursdays and Saturdays, landing at Washington just before lunchtime. All services continue on south to Miami, Florida. Return flights depart mid-mornings on Wednesdays, Fridays and Sundays. A complimentary limousine service is provided for transfer between Washington's Dulles and National Airports. Concorde is also used on some seasonal schedules to Barbados.

Below:

Mach 1 (the speed of sound) is reached at 29,000ft. The light grey upholstery and white luggage racks and ceiling panels give the cabin a spacious appearance. The central bulkhead has also done much to eliminate the 'tube' effect of the narrow fuselage.
Author

Left:
In October 1968 BEA began a programme to convert nine Vanguard airliners to Merchantmen freighters, with cargo doors and other modifications. Photographed here in 1979, a British Airways Cargo Merchantman climbs away from Heathrow Airport.
Anthony Wirkus

Below:
The last Cambrian Airways types, the Viscount and One-Eleven, at their home base at Cardiff. Both became part of the British Airways fleet after integration. *Austin J. Brown*

Far left:
Trident 1E of Northeast Airlines, formerly BKS Air Transport, was a frequent visitor to Newcastle until the company became part of British Airways.
Ian MacFarlane

Left:
BOAC's order for the American Boeing 707-436 was the subject of much controversy amongst the 'Buy British' lobby in the late 1950s. *Anthony Wirkus*

On 1 January 1983, Concorde made its fastest-ever crossing of the North Atlantic by covering the New York-London run in 2hrs 56min 35sec. The westbound record stands at 3hrs 11min.

The average load factor on scheduled services is now approaching 80% and, whilst this appears just a little too high for comfort, Concorde passengers rarely have to be turned away even from peak services, as there is also a high 'no-show' of 10%. This is due largely to the complete flexibility of a Concorde ticket which has no restrictive elements and is valid for 12 months, thus allowing the businessman the luxury to change his mind and his flight up to the last minute. With lower fuel prices and consequently a reduced break-even load factor including all incurred costs of some 50%, the new profitability of Concorde becomes evident.

The Star Attraction

Wherever Concorde makes an appearance it invariably becomes the star attraction, and to date the British Airways fleet has visited destinations in 80 countries around the world – and the list is still growing. While business travel remains the primary market, the demand over recent years for luxury leisure travel has developed to such an extent that the seventh aircraft was returned to flying duties and there are times when British Airways could do with one or two more.

Concorde charters take many forms and have included such varied activities as official government flights, visits to air shows and trade fairs and serving as a viewing platform while chasing Halley's Comet across the Indian Ocean. Highlight to date has undoubtedly been the special occasion in August 1985 when Her Majesty Queen Elizabeth the Queen Mother travelled on Concorde around the British coastline at the invitation of British Airways to mark her 85th birthday.

A regular series of one-and-a-half-hour supersonic flights, dubbed the 'Champagne Specials', is now available from British Airways for just £350. This includes a champagne lunch in flight, supersonic certificate and Concorde souvenir and information packs. As the cheapest single ticket on the scheduled three-and-a-half-hour transatlantic services is currently fixed at £1,442, these special charters represent exceptional value and bring a supersonic trip in Concorde, which for many would be a once-in-a-lifetime experience, within the compass of a greater number of people. Round-the-world tours were also offered by a tour company during 1986 and 1987 and will continue in 1988. The first such charter completed 30,000 miles (50,000km) in a flying time of just over 30hrs, calling at New York, Oakland, Honolulu, Guam, Hong Kong, Bali, Colombo, Bahrain and Cairo.

It has been said that, short of flying to the moon, circling the world on Concorde is the absolute ultimate in jet-set travel.

The Look

The striking new Concorde look was created by Landor Associates in conjunction with Chester Jones and Gretchen Bellinger as part of the most recent overall change in the British Airways corporate image. It was introduced in December 1984 and features the red Speedwing running down the length of the fuselage and the airline's coat of arms on the tail fin. The latter is set against the quartered Union Jack in a midnight blue background at the top half of the fin. Unlike the rest of the British Airways fleet, however, Concorde has an all-white fuselage to reflect the heat and to minimise the high surface temperature of the airframe experienced while flying at supersonic speeds. Luxurious passenger seats – upholstered in high-grade leather and limousine cloth in delicate shades of grey, with toning leather on the bulkheads and carpets of a similar colour – combine with soft lighting and white side panels and overhead luggage racks, to create a restful and co-ordinated interior. The tube effect of the necessarily narrow fuselage is often commented on, but has been virtually eliminated by the lighter interior and by the installation of a central galley area which breaks up the length into two cabins of 40 seats in the forward fuselage and 60 seats at the rear. Seating arrangement is two-abreast with a central isle.

The interior colour scheme is carried through to the table settings with white bone china edged with platinum and black, complemented by the clean and unfussy lines of the stainless steel cutlery and high-quality glassware. To complete the table settings there are crisp white damask tablecloths and napkins.

A computerised display on the bulkhead at the front of each cabin welcomes passengers to Concorde; during the flight it provides continuous information of the Mach number, altitude, outside air temperature and true air speeds in mph. The 'distance to go' can also be displayed in place of the temperature.

The Operation

Concorde does not require special facilities or support services when on the ground, but makes much more demands on the flight crew – especially during take-off – where there is twice the work to be done, concentrated into a shorter period. This is particularly true at JFK where there are a number of restrictions with regard to crossing height and banking angles among others. Operationally, Concorde is basically two aircraft, subsonic and supersonic, each with its own specific workload. The fact that unlike more modern aircraft, Concorde technology is analogue rather than digital, also places additional burdens on the crew.

Once out over the sea, Concorde climbs steadily to its typical cruising altitude of between 50,000 and 60,000ft (15,000 and 18,250m) and a speed of Mach 2. This is maintained for some 2hrs of the crossing, though depending on the prevailing air temperatures, the true airspeed at twice the speed of sound may vary from 1,300 to 1,470mph (2,100 to 2,370km/h).

At these very high speeds of operations, even allowing for a typical air temperature of −60°C (−76°F) 11 miles up, Concorde is subject to frictional heating which raises the external skin temperature up to +127°C (260°F). The resultant expansion, stretching the fuselage a full 10in (250mm) in flight, is taken up by specially developed aluminium alloys used for its construction. Neither this excessive heat, nor the sizeable lengthening of the structure, is discernible inside the cabin environment due to the special sandwich construction which enhances the insulation against the heat, and an independent floor on rollers which absorbs the expansion. There are, however, a few telltale signs to be discovered. The passenger can detect the exceptional heat passing through the structure when touching the inner layer of Perspex over the small cabin window, as it is not possible to achieve comparable insulation values with translucent materials. A strikingly visual manifestation of Concorde's expansion is a gap − large enough to allow a man's hand to pass in sideways during cruise at Mach 2 − which appears at the rear of the flight engineer's panel. This gap closes almost completely when the aircraft is back on the ground. Some 165 miles (260km) from the coast, Concorde begins to slow down from Mach 2 to reach Mach 1, making the change from supersonic to subsonic speed at a minimum of 55 miles (90km) out to meet stringent UK and US requirements. As the emotive sonic boom actually occurs some 30 miles (48km) ahead of the aircraft, this still leaves a 25-mile (42km) buffer zone. Like other aircraft in the British Airways fleet, Concorde is capable of fully-automatic landing to the advanced Category III standard with forward visibility of only 250ft (75m).

With an equivalent altitude of 6,000ft (1,800m) when cruising at 58,000ft (17,500m), the cabin environment is pressurised to a much more comfortable altitude than on subsonic aircraft, reducing in-flight fatigue. However, the major fatigue saving results from the considerably reduced journey times relative to the distance covered, which ensures that the traveller arrives at his destination fresh and relaxed.

The Engineering
Where Concorde is concerned, cost is always uppermost in the mind. Not only are its maintenance man-hour costs about four times that of a Boeing 747, each spare part has a similarly inflated price tag due to the fact that only a few aircraft are flying and purchase costs were artificially loaded by the government to enable it to recover some of the large expenditure incurred in building the aircraft. Even so, British Airways has achieved the seemingly impossible by managing to operate Concorde at a profit. Another significant aspect with regard to engineering are the complexities inherent in an aircraft which is now more than 20 years old. With all the superlatives heaped on Concorde, it seems rather strange to label it as old technology, but such it is in spite of state-of-the-art features which include fly-by-wire.

Maintenance is a complicated procedure and when technical problems do occur, they also tend to affect the whole fleet at the same time, requiring particular attention and increased effort. The same engineers, therefore, look after the aircraft from the moment it arrives on the ramp to the actual departure, and this has generated a tremendous team spirit among the engineers and a close working relationship with the technical crews and other, non-engineering, staff.

Concorde engineers have been responsible for well over 300 modifications since the aircraft entered service. The great majority of these have been carried out to improve reliability − especially despatch reliability, which now averages 95% − appearance and passenger amenities. The perfect safety record of Concorde in more than 11 years of scheduled service speaks volumes for the skill and dedication of the engineering team. It will not be a lack of either, nor advancing years, but a drying up of spare parts, which will eventually force the grounding of the Concorde fleet. That day though, is yet a long way in the future.

The Team
Apart from administrative staff, the flight crew complement comprises 22 captains and an equal number of first officers and flight engineers. All have been selected after long years of experience at the controls of subsonic jets and now fly exclusively on Concorde. Cabin staff, totalling some 200, rotate between Concorde, Boeing 737s and BAC One-Elevens. As a single sector flight does not exceed three-and-a-half hours, Concorde, alongside these other types, is classified as a short/medium-haul aircraft.

The crews operate a 28-day duty roster working six days on and three days off, which means that each team makes six to seven round trips a month. Every Concorde flight carries nine crew: captain, first officer, flight engineer and six cabin staff under the supervision of a flight services director.

London/New York/London by Concorde

The Only Way to Fly
The dream which had taken shape in the distant memories of 1969 when Concorde made its first-ever flight, was at last about to become reality. No queuing at the check-in, a leisurely amble through passport control and security check, time and space to admire the new terminal along the way. 'Was this the real way to fly?' I mused, still with both feet on the ground. Speedwing signs pointed the way to the Concorde Lounge and the height of luxury with deep pile carpets, upholstered furniture one does not want to get up from, telephones, television and a bar that had everything. As it was too early for me, a black coffee and Danish pastry had to suffice, though others were less reticent in pouring themselves double whiskies before slumping into comfortable armchairs to read their favourite newspaper, also freely available. A slight diversion by

British Airways in the Making — 3

Left:
The Hawker Siddeley Trident rear-engined tri-jet formed the main fleet of BEA during the 1960s and 1970s, and was finally retired from British Airways service in 1985.
Anthony Wirkus

Right:
Perhaps one of the most elegant airliners to have flown the British Airways flag, the Vickers Super VC-10 enabled the airline to consolidate its route network across the globe during the 1960s.
Anthony Wirkus

Left:
A cargo version of the Boeing 707 featured a large freight-loading door in the forward fuselage. *Anthony Wirkus*

Below left:
First flown in 1963, the BAC One-Eleven still gives sterling service on some of British Airways' thinner routes. Super One-Eleven G-AVMN is pictured at Manchester in September 1979.
Anthony Wirkus

Below:
The wide-bodied Boeing 737 represented an exciting new addition to British Airways' short-haul fleet in the 1970s. This example was on loan from the Dutch operator Transavia during 1979.
Anthony Wirkus

Above:
A Concorde flight begins at the luxurious Speedwing Lounge in Terminal 4 under the watchful eyes of the magnificent white bird.
British Airways/Adrian Meredith

British Airways Market Research enquiring about my smoking (or in this case non-smoking) habits, before appetising sandwiches offered by efficient lounge staff made renewed appeals to my stomach. Concorde G-BOAB invitingly pointed its long nose towards the window but, surrounded by airport paraphernalia, was rather too shy to be photographed.

Twenty minutes to take-off and we were politely invited to board the aircraft, just a few steps away from the lounge. Mike Bannister, Senior First Officer, volunteered the information that our flight would be under the command of Captain John Hutchinson, that our flight time would be 3hrs and 23min and that we would be cruising at 54,000ft. Once we had cleared the Bristol Channel, Concorde would be accelerating to twice the speed of sound.

'Would you like a glass of champagne after take-off, sir?' I could not think of a single reason why I should turn down such a friendly offer. At 10.54, from a standing start on runway 28R, now 27R, Concorde with full reheat from its enormous engines, accelerated away like the thoroughbred it is, becoming airborne at 10.55 and climbing steadily, leaving Heathrow, the Staines reservoirs and Windsor Castle far below. The cabin was a little more noisy, though not excessively so, and the slight shudder experienced on take-off soon died away.

There was no time at all for admiring the landscape under the huge delta wing below, nor to keep a note of the fast-changing facts and figures on the digital display, before my glass was being filled with *Cuvée de René Lalou Millesime*, followed immediately by smoked salmon, cheese mosaic and paupiette of sole canapés served on a snow-white damask tablecloth. For the next two hours we were wined and dined and treated like VIPs by cabin staff whose unobtrusive efficiency and friendliness were offered in equal measure. Delicious food prepared with surprising creativity included an appetiser of fresh mangos, a choice of three main courses (I tried the Concorde Brunch of grilled Kasseler steak, pork sausages garnished

with mushroom and tomatoes, rösti potatoes and mixed salad), followed with fresh seasonal woodland berries in champagne jelly. Taylor's Vintage Port helped to ease down a selection from the cheeseboard, and coffee, handmade chocolates and one (or maybe two) glasses of Irish Cream, brought this veritable feast to a warming close. Amazingly, the flight was almost over. The digital flight display indicated that we had broken the sound barrier at 30,000ft – though there was no sensation of having done so inside the cabin. Mach 2 – twice the speed of sound – was reached at 49,500ft, 1hr 16min after take-off, and soon after our cruising altitude, almost 10 miles up where the sun always shines and the clouds below are puffy white and pretty. With less than 200 miles to go, the speed was being reduced and we began the descent over Jamaica Bay, touching down at Kennedy Airport after the shortest long distance flight ever. Customs formalities were quickly completed and New York Helicopters staff accompanied several passengers to the Sikorsky S-58, a short bus-ride away for the transfer to downtown New York. The large square windows afforded the first close-up view of the famed Manhattan skyline from the air, before we landed smoothly at the East 34th Street Heliport on the Hudson River some 10 minutes later. An incredible four hours after leaving the ground at London, I found myself almost 4,000 miles away in the heart of the 'Big Apple'.

The return flight in G-BOAA was under the command of Captain Harry Linfield, assisted by Senior First Officer Derek Whitton and Flight Engineer Bill Hornby, all self-confessed Concorde enthusiasts. The invitation to visit the flightdeck was accepted with eager anticipation and from that vantage point, climbing out over the green isles and white sandy beaches of Jamaica Bay, was as spectacular a sight as any I had seen. Beyond Nantucket Island, Concorde accelerated towards maximum speed and its homeward cruising altitude of 58,000ft. More of the same pampering with different but equally delicious culinary delights, made the time fly as the saying goes – twice as fast on Concorde – and we were soon passing the Welsh coast, Plymouth, Exeter, Lyneham, descending at a rate of 1,000ft every 15sec.

Another aircraft on approach was having difficulty finding the correct runway. 'He probably got lost looking at the sights', commented air traffic control. And it was easy to see why: London on a clear night was something special to behold and even the crew, for whom this was anything but a new experience, had difficulty in deciding whether to keep their eyes on the orange and white lights below, or on the flightdeck controls. The nose and visor were dropped and the runway lights were clearly visible in the rapidly shrinking distance. A smooth touchdown was made 3hrs and 19min after leaving New York. Reverse thrust slowed Concorde down dramatically before it turned off the runway and towards the terminal.

The flight, the experience, the dream was over. The reality will remain forever.

5 British Airways Nationwide – Has Britain Covered

It would be quite wrong to think of British Airways only in terms of its well-publicised profile as Britain's international airline carrying the flag to more countries around the world than any other airline. It is a fact that British Airways also has by far the most extensive scheduled services network within the United Kingdom, with more than 1,000 flights a week, serving 15 destinations. Five million people – or one in four of all British Airways passengers – travel on a domestic flight.

This wide coverage of the British Isles is achieved through the implementation of four distinct service sectors: Super Shuttle, Trunk Routes, Regional Services and Highlands Division. Super Shuttle and Trunk Routes are those services providing frequent direct nonstop flights between London and major provincial cities, while these same cities are linked across country with each other to form an integrated regional network pattern. Regional airports benefit further through a growing number of direct connections to international destinations. Highlands Division was set up principally to serve the Highlands and islands of Scotland, but has now expanded its activities much further afield.

The domestic fleet is based on the advanced Boeing 757 and also comprises the popular 737 and One-Eleven jets, as well as the HS 748 turboprop aircraft. All are twin-engined machines with a capacity ranging from 44 seats in the HS 748 to 195 seats in the Boeing 757. Eight BAe ATPs will join the fleet from November 1988.

Super Shuttle

Super Service

The shuttle concept, still unique in Europe, provides a guaranteed seat without prior reservation to any full fare-paying passenger. This guarantee entails a readiness to provide a back-up aircraft for each service even if there is only a single passenger who cannot be accommodated on the first aircraft. Shuttle was originally introduced into British Airways in 1975 and has carried almost 20 million passengers in the 12 years since. The introduction of a competitive service by British Midland Airways on some routes in 1981/82 forced British Airways into a fundamental re-evaluation of its product. In September 1983 it relaunched its service as the Super Shuttle offering substantial improvements, particularly the provision of breakfast on morning services and free bar and hot beverages with light snacks throughout the day. The Super Shuttle proved a resounding success and the British Airways market share quickly recovered lost ground.

British Airways Super Shuttle routes serve four major cities with high frequency flight direct from Heathrow, providing up to 12 flights a day to Glasgow and Manchester, 10 to Edinburgh and seven to Belfast. The same number of daily connections are also scheduled in the opposite direction. Advanced technology Boeing 757s are used on most services, supplemented on some off-peak schedules and on other occasions by BAC One-Elevens and Boeing 737s. To the surprise and unexpected delight of many passengers, even Concorde has made rare appearances on the Super Shuttle routes. All aircraft are fitted with Autoland and are capable of landing in low-visibility weather conditions, thus adding enhanced regularity to the other benefits.

Dedicated Super Shuttle facilities are located at Heathrow's Terminal 1 and include ticket offices, check-in desks and a well-equipped lounge with seating for 300 passengers, bar, buffet, teletext television and electronic news display. The 2m x 1m board delivers the latest news direct from the Press Association and for the businessman/woman especially, also displays the *Financial Times*

Left:
Leading from the front: the impressive bulk of a Boeing 747. *Anthony Wirkus*

Below:
A Boeing 747 in the old British Airways colours landing in front of the Wardair hangars at Toronto International Airport, Canada, in August 1983. *Transport Canada*

Bottom:
Tails of success: a line-up of five British Airways Boeing 747s bearing a mixture of old and new liveries. *British Airways*

Index, the gold price and the latest Dollar/Sterling exchange rate.

Check-in for passengers without hold baggage is a mere 10min and seat selection is arranged in the lounge itself. Once on the aircraft, a drink and free morning (or evening) papers are offered, together with a full breakfast consisting of rolls, coffee, fruit juice and cooked main course on all departures up to 09.30hrs. On the shorter Manchester route there is only time for a continental breakfast. Avis self-service car rental facilities in the Super Shuttle lounges in all five cities ensure a 'fast getaway'. One-stop check-in is available at Glasgow, Edinburgh and Manchester for onward international British Airways flights at Heathrow. Another benefit, exclusive to Shuttle passengers, is a special monthly theatre and sports entertainment brochure which features major events and entertainment in London and the regions, together with a priority credit card booking number.

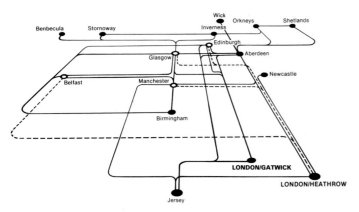

Domestic route diagram

A simple fare structure comprising the normal Super Shuttle fare, Super Shuttle Saver, Super Shuttle Early Saver and Super Shuttle Standby, offers the traveller a wide-ranging choice of flights and/or price and helps to stimulate demand on off-peak flights. An Early Saver Return, by way of an example, costs only a fraction more than a standard single ticket. A major convenience, especially for the business traveller in a hurry, is the British Airways Time Saver Ticket. This enables the traveller to write out his or her own ticket immediately after having booked the flight by telephone (not necessary, of course, on Super Shuttle routes) quoting a British Airways account number. Time Savers are available in books of 10 easy-to-use blank flight tickets and can be used on all domestic services.

In 1987/8 over 3 million passengers travelled on the four British Airways Super Shuttle routes, alone producing some 65% of the total UK domestic traffic. Number one destination is Manchester, followed by Glasgow, both supporting in excess of 1 million passengers, Belfast and Edinburgh.

London Trunk Routes

In addition to the Super Shuttle services, British Airways operates three major scheduled trunk routes from Heath-

46

row, northwards to Aberdeen and Newcastle and south to the financial and holiday centre of Jersey in the Channel Islands. Up to seven flights a day with full meal services at appropriate times are currently scheduled to Aberdeen – Scotland's 'oil city' – and to Newcastle – regional capital and industrial centre of the northeast. A large proportion of the total traffic to both these cities (half a million at Aberdeen and a quarter of a million at Newcastle) are transit passengers, using these services to reach other cross-country destinations, as well as the oil and gas fields in the North Sea. Jersey has five special daily services where passengers are treated to free champagne. This route which caters largely for the holiday maker, supports a quarter of a million passengers a year. BAC One-Elevens and Boeing 737s share services on all three trunk routes with the larger Boeing 757 substituting on peak schedules between London and Aberdeen. Aberdeen, Glasgow, Edinburgh and Jersey also have frequent direct British Airways connections from London Gatwick. All are flown with One-Elevens and depart from the South Terminal.

Manchester International Airport is the busiest and by a substantial margin British Airways' biggest operating base outside London. Situated in the heart of the industrial region, the airport's catchment area extends from the Midlands and throughout the North of England serving a potential 20 million people and almost half the country's entire manufacturing industry. The future provision of a rail link, serving the passenger terminals from the near BR InterCity station, will further consolidate the airport's position as a major northern gateway. Recognising its importance, British Airways has put down strong roots with a deliberate policy to further strengthen its presence and to continue to build up its services at Manchester.

Of more than 130 destinations now served regularly by air, British Airways is responsible for nearly 40% and the 1.75 million scheduled and charter passengers carried in and out of Manchester each year account for more than 25% of the airport's total traffic. As the leading handling agents at the airport, British Airways also looks after another 1.25 million passengers, serving many other airlines.

Extensive jet services are operated to British, European and intercontinental destinations. In the UK – Birmingham, Belfast, Glasgow, Aberdeen, Jersey and London/Heathrow are all served with frequent daily flights. An ever-increasing number of European destinations include Amsterdam, Athens, Brussels, Copenhagen, Cork, Dublin, Dusseldorf, Frankfurt, Geneva, Hamburg, Hannover, Malta, Milan, Munich, Nice, Paris, Stockholm and Rome. Long-haul flights are operated to New York, Barbados, Orlando, Bombay, Delhi and Hong Kong. New York is served daily with Boeing 747s and frequency on the Manchester-Hong Kong route is twice weekly, with one flight a week serving the two Indian cities. Whilst the most recent developments have taken place in the scheduled services field, British

Airways also has ambitious plans for a considerable expansion of its holiday operations. Alongside Gatwick, Manchester is already a principal base for British Airways' inclusive tour company which offers an extensive annual jet programme of 40,000-plus continental holidays out of Manchester. The Poundstretcher subsidiary provides some 20,000 transatlantic seats on 747 charters to North America, serving Toronto, New York, New Orleans and Los Angeles. Cargo is another growth area and in March 1986 British Airways completed a brand-new £7 million terminal regarded as the best-equipped anywhere in Great Britain. The new facilities will enable British Airways to double its present throughput at Manchester of about 30,000 tonnes a year. Scheduled transatlantic and Far East services make up most of this tonnage, but cargo space is also available on 747 summer charters to the United States and Canada.

Birmingham

Midlands Hub

Birmingham's position in the centre of England's motorway system, an InterCity railway station and the successful National Exhibition Centre at its doorstep, together with the opening of new facilities in 1984, have propelled Birmingham International towards being a major airport hub for links with its EEC trading partners. British Airways has a long association with Birmingham going back to postwar years and it is now firmly established as an important regional base, from which it operates a continually expanding pattern of services to other British cities and to important business centres on the continent and the Irish Republic. A fleet of six One-Elevens and 400 staff are based locally, supporting some half-a-million passengers annually on British Airways routes in and out of Birmingham.

There is no doubt of the benefits that British Airways services bring to the Midlands community, but Birmingham is also developing fast as a major interchange where passengers from Scotland, Ireland and continental Europe are offered convenient onward connections.

Scheduled British Airways services currently link Birmingham with Glasgow, Edinburgh, Aberdeen, Manchester and Belfast and outside the United Kingdom with Amsterdam, Dusseldorf, Frankfurt, Hannover, Munich, Malaga, Paris, Dublin and Cork. New routes will be added as the market develops. In addition to scheduled services British Airways also flies holiday charters mainly to Mediterranean destinations.

British Airways Highlands Division

The Highlands Division was launched in April 1982 as a much slimmed-down version of the Scottish operations which had been provided by British Airways and its predecessors since 1947. Headquarters are at Glasgow Airport even though the largest staff (out of a total of 200)

and a great deal of the activity is centred at Aberdeen, Scotland's 'oil capital'. Day-to-day control and all engineering for its fleet is maintained at Glasgow Airport.

A total of twelve HS 748 twin-turboprops are currently in service including five model 2Bs which are owned by British Airways, one 2A on a long-term lease from Dan-Air, three on lease from DLT and three more 2As leased from Euroair. In addition to 44 passenger seats, there is plenty of room for baggage, newspapers, mail and freight – an important element of the service – and this capacity, together with an excellent operating performance makes the aircraft ideal for the present route structure in Scotland. There are times, however, when a larger aircraft could be used on specific routes and frequencies and the BAe ATP has been ordered for delivery commencing in November 1988. The 748s carry some 300,000 passengers per year and the total to date exceeds 1.5 million passengers at an average load factor of 60%. The Division presently has 105 flight crew comprising 46 Captains and 59 First Officers, under the management of Flight Manager Captain Colin Seaman. All are volunteers from the mainline operation, typically First Officers from such types as the 737, One-Eleven and the now withdrawn Trident. A total of 44 cabin staff, based at either Glasgow or Aberdeen, have been drawn mainly from other, ground-based, British Airways occupations. Each flight carries two flight crew and one steward/stewardess.

The Scottish services of the Highlands Division are based on the two hubs of Glasgow and Aberdeen, reflecting its route structure to and from the Western and Northern Isles respectively. From Glasgow there are nonstop flights from a single frequency to three services a day to Aberdeen, Inverness, Benbecula and Stornoway (Isle of Lewis), and nonstop services from Aberdeen are flown to Edinburgh, Glasgow, Wick, Kirkwall (Orkney) and Sumburgh (Shetland). Stornoway also has a direct link to Inverness and there is an inter-island connection between Orkney and Shetland. A summer service extends from the latter across the North Sea to Bergen, servicing the North Sea energy sector and maintaining the historic links between Scotland and Norway.

Other Highlands Division routes are flown from Scotland to Belfast, Birmingham and Manchester, with weekend services from Birmingham to Cork; Manchester to Münster/Osnabrück and, in summer only, Aberdeen to Jersey. 748s are also utilised on internal German services operating between Berlin/Tegel and Münster/Osnabrück, Hannover and Bremen, with weekend sectors to Düsseldorf. Mainline connections are available at Glasgow, Aberdeen and Edinburgh to the rest of the UK and to points in Europe.

The Highlands Division also offers a selection of interesting holiday packages to the Northern Isles, and sightseeing flights over the Highlands and islands also keep the 748s busy at the weekends. In addition to the normal Saver, Early Saver and Standby fares, a special low-cost Highland Rover ticket is available which allows up to eight flights within Scotland over a period of up to 14 days.

Concorde — The Best of British

Above:
The apron of Manchester International Airport is shared by four different types including a British Airways Concorde and a Boeing 757.
Manchester Airport/Paul Francis Photography

Right:
High over the Atlantic en route route to New York, Concorde flight engineer Bill Hornby monitors the aircraft's systems.
Allan Burney

Above left:
Passengers are treated to the best in catering including fine vintage wines and excellent champagnes. *Allan Burney*

Above:
The Concorde crew are briefed 1½hr before departure. *Allan Burney*

Left:
British Airways Concorde at Heathrow's Terminal 4.
Arthur Kemsley

An Airline Within An Airline

When Gerry Devine, Manager of the British Airways Highlands Division, was thrust into a planning role in the 25-strong working group that proposed the creation of the Division in October 1981 to turn round the ailing Scottish operations, little did he realise that he would later have the opportunity to put theory into practice. That was in 1981 and today he professes himself quietly pleased with progress to date – the Division is profitable and expanding – and confident for the future. They are quick to point out, however, that there remains much still to be done. A similar attitude and perception of the work in hand has been noticeable throughout all the staff encountered – enthusiasm, enjoyment and job satisfaction, but at the same time always a willingness to seek improvements and to face new challenges.

Success owes much to the flexible working practices within the Division which, although forced upon it as a result of drastic cutbacks in staff in 1982, have been accepted as the only way forward and now serve as an example to other companies with similar operations, many of whom have visited to find out how it is done. It is not unusual to see the flight captain helping out with baggage loading, stewards checking in passengers and a wide range of other tasks being performed as the necessity arises, by whoever is in the right place at the right time.

The Highlands Division enjoys a fair degree of autonomy from London and is very much an airline within an airline, being allowed to apply its local expertise to the benefit of British Airways as a whole. It makes use of mainline support services on a normal repayment basis and is subject to the same high standards of operation as elsewhere within British Airways. There is unconcealed pride that within a strict commercial framework, the Division is able to provide a vital community service to the Scottish people, and in so doing has become a respected part of the local scene.

Flight BA5822 under the command of Captain Dave Baker, assisted by First Officer Ray Howell and Steward Don McEachern, was being readied for the second of two daily flights to Stornoway on the Isle of Lewis in the Outer Hebrides. There was time to have a quick word with Captain Baker who, like his colleagues in the Division, is a 748 enthusiast. He is also the last of the original 748 pilots in Scotland, having made the switch from Tridents to the twin turboprops – affectionately christened 'Budgies' – in 1975.

Although he has flown this route many times, the scenery when visible below the Scottish mist, is still for him one of the highlights of this route. The vagaries of the weather in these parts make flying a much more demanding and consequently, he assured me, a more enjoyable experience, especially combined with the confidence inspired by the ruggedness and reliability of the aircraft. When flying into Stornoway, local knowledge is invaluable, with low clouds and high winds – sometimes in tandem – proving the greatest menace to man and machine. Similar conditions prevail on the other routes, but on this flight it was difficult to imagine.

After taking off from rainy Glasgow, the sudden unexpected breaks in the cloud cover afforded a splendid view of Loch Lomond and the Isle of Mull before we headed north, passing the Isle of Skye on the crossing of the North Minch Channel towards Stornoway. After a one-hour flight in bright sunshine, the landing at the 2,100m runway – the longest in the Scottish Isles – was accomplished with hardly a bump, and within minutes disembarkation of the 25 passengers was completed. The flight crew disappeared into the tiny office of Station Manager Alex MacRae to complete their paperwork and prepare for the next sector to Inverness. Whilst three men struggled to unload a 160kg crate of generator spares (100kg is the normal limit as there are no mechanical means at the airport) Don McEachern made himself busy checking in a full load of passengers for the onward flight. For Alex MacRae, D.R. MacDonald and Donnie MacKenzie, the only British Airways staff at the airport, the arrival of the 748 also marked the beginning of a hectic period, although there is never a really quiet time, even with only four daily services into Stornoway – two by British Airways and two by Loganair. There is additionally some military activity as the airport, although managed by the CAA, is RAF property and part of a wide range of facilities on the island for use by forces of the Western Alliance. Its location near the northern approaches also makes it of paramount strategic importance.

An ambulance arrived and a young mother boarded the plane carrying her seven-week-old baby to Inverness for a specialist operation at Raigmore Hospital. When no suitable medical facilities exist on the island, patients are issued with a 'hospital ticket' by the DHSS for flights to the mainland. Speed is often of the essence and, by comparison with flying (40min to Inverness, 60min to Glasgow), a trip to Glasgow by boat (if the weather allows) and car, can take at least 12 hours. Another important regular visitor, and one on which the islanders depend for keeping in touch, is the red Royal Mail van.

BA5833 departed on time, half-an-hour after landing at Stornoway for its 40min flight to Inverness. With 44 passengers Don had his hands full, but by the time we arrived everyone had been served with a free drink and a friendly word or two. Many were old friends and the community spirit was there for all to see. In contrast to our flight to Stornoway, heavy cloud cover prevented any view of the Highlands or the Loch Ness monster, but a glimpse of the Moray Firth on approach was worth the wait. After a brief stop-over and a change of aircraft and crew, BA5723 took us back to Glasgow.

The islanders, not only in Stornoway, but also at Benbecula, Orkney and Shetland, have come to rely on British Airways at all times of the year, in fair weather and foul, and the weather can be so disagreeable that even the seagulls are grounded. It is to the great credit of all the staff of the Highlands Division that the 'Budgies' continue to fly.

6 British Airways – Passport to Europe

A British Airways ticket truly is a passport to Europe, its service tentacles spreading out to all but a handful of countries, reaching 60 points, including virtually every leading European city. Of these, the Irish Sea crossings to Cork (daily), Shannon (daily) and Dublin (seven times a day), have figured strongly since the 1930s in supporting trade between the two countries.

British Airways has generally made great inroads into the European business travel market, although tourism has by no means been neglected. This is noticeable by the rapid development of scheduled 'leisure' routes flown to the Mediterranean sunspots, mainly out of London/Gatwick and a growing list of provincial airports.

The vast majority of the routes are now operated by the Boeing 757 and 737 twin jets, Airbus A320 and the Lockheed TriStar, with relatively few services still flown by the smaller One-Elevens. The introduction in 1983 of the advanced 757 made possible considerable improvements in punctuality and service standards, and led directly to the sparkling success of British Airways' Club Europe, now available to all destinations throughout Europe. Designed to appeal to the businessman who was increasingly looking for improved standards of service without having to pay the full First Class fare on short trips,

Below:
The vast majority of European routes are now operated by the Boeing 737 (top) and 757 twin jets.
British Airways/Adrian Meredith

Salzburg Airport, Austria, taken over by British Airtours TriStars and Boeing 737s during a wintry March day in 1986. A British Airways Boeing 737 is also there.
Salzburg Airport

Flagships of the European fleet are the Lockheed TriStar (below) and the Boeing 757 (right), two of the technically most advanced aircraft.
British Airways/Adrian Meredith and Boeing

The different TriStar models are employed on a multitude of services ranging from short, high-density to long-haul scheduled routes and inclusive tour work. The aircraft pictured now flies in Caledonian Airways colours named 'Loch Earne'. *Salzburg Airport*

A Boeing 757 at a wet Zürich Airport, Switzerland. In addition to Zürich, British Airways also serves Basle and Geneva.
Flughafen Zürich

Club traffic has risen steadily and is now approaching 2 million passengers a year. Or, put another way, an impressive 25% of all passengers carried on the airline's European routes. In addition to exclusive check-in facilities, increased baggage allowance and in-flight complimentary services, Club travel also offers the convenience of a fully-flexible late access ticket to provide maximum assistance to the business traveller whose plans change at short notice.

Services to Europe also enjoy a good reputation for punctuality with 85% of all British Airways European services leaving Heathrow within 15min of their scheduled departure time.

The British Airways share of European airline traffic has increased to 8 million passengers a year, carried on over 800 return flights a week. Very roughly, this works out at 100 passengers per flight.

All the signs point to a continued gradual upward movement of traffic, but substantial progress in this direction is not likely until the advent of the 'Free Market' in 1992.

Germany Above All – Almost

Two distinct markets, domestic and international together with long-haul sales and cargo, form British Airways' third largest trading area in the world, behind only the UK and North Atlantic operations. On up to 120 flights per day, the airline carries over 2.5 million passengers a year into, out of, or within Germany. Of these, some 1.2 million scheduled passengers travel between Germany and the UK, this figure being made up of 60% business and 40% non-business traffic. This impressive total has been achieved in spite of fierce competition from Lufthansa, Pan American and many other national airlines having full traffic rights between the two countries. The German market area contributes an annual revenue now exceeding £120 million. Scheduled operations comprise more than 50 sector flights daily between six UK and nine German cities. From London/Heathrow, British Airways flies direct to Düsseldorf, Frankfurt, Hamburg, Munich, Stuttgart, Bremen, Hannover, Cologne/Bonn and, of course, to Berlin. Manchester is similarly linked into the system with direct connections to Frankfurt, Munich, Hamburg, Hannover and Düsseldorf; the last-named also has a scheduled service from Jersey in the Channel Islands. The growing importance of Scotland and the Midlands to trade with the EEC has been recognised with their own German connections from Glasgow, Edinburgh and Birmingham to Frankfurt, Düsseldorf and Hannover. Aircraft used are Boeing 757s and 737s and BAC One-Elevens.

Since July 1984 British Airways has offered Club travel for full Economy fare passengers at no extra charge on all routes between Germany and the UK. This has proved very popular and accounts for the present high figure of around 50% of Club Europe travellers which is expected to rise still further. Red Saver Fares, comparable to cheap charter rates are also available on a large number of selected services to all destinations, as are

short-stay fly-drive holiday packages to West Berlin and other German destinations.

The Internal German Services (IGS) network was established soon after the Berlin Airlift in 1948/49 during which BEA played a prominent part in co-ordinating the British effort, a fact often forgotten. The years since have seen a gradual development of routes, upgrading of equipment from Vikings, Elizabethans and Viscounts to Super One-Elevens and now Boeing 737s, as well as operational moves from Berlin-Gatow to Tempelhof and finally to Tegel Airport. Today British Airways provides direct services from Berlin to eight destinations in the Federal Republic.

Principal IGS routes – and among the oldest – are those to the Rhine cities of Düsseldorf and Cologne/Bonn, first introduced on 1 December 1949 and 26 September 1950 respectively. Boeing 737s fly both routes seven times throughout the day, largely carrying industrial and commercial business traffic. Also in operation for more than 25 years is the Berlin-Hannover link, at 40min the shortest of the IGS routes. Opened on 12 June 1950, this service is presently scheduled six times a day. The longest by contrast, with a scheduled time of 75min, is Berlin-Stuttgart, opened with Vickers Viscounts on 1 June 1965. Current frequency is five flights a day in each direction. The Berlin-Bremen route goes back to 1 April 1964, since when it has been flown almost entirely with high-capacity jet aircraft. The introduction on 19 May 1986 of two 44-seat HS 748 turboprop aircraft enabled the sought-after increase in frequency, giving passengers a choice of four flights a day both ways with more during the summer.

Frequency on the Berlin-Münster/Osnabrück service (first flown on 29 October 1984) has also been improved with the 748 by adding a midday flight to the peak morning and evening schedule. A connection from Münster/Osnabrück to Glasgow via Manchester is available on Sundays. The latest addition to the network is a four times a day routing to Munich. Between April and October, one daily flight leaves Berlin mid-morning for Westerland on the Frisian island of Sylt, the Germans' favourite summer resort in the North Sea. After a brief stop-over, the 737 completes the 60min return journey by early afternoon.

Germany's importance to British Airways is not confined to traffic within Germany or between the two countries, but also extends to a sizeable feeder element for its transatlantic routes to the USA, Caribbean and South America.

The other German-speaking countries of Austria and Switzerland also feature well in British Airways' European activities, highlighted by a strong business element and supported by some of the best summer and winter leisure attractions on the continent. Switzerland, after Germany and France, is British Airways' major business market commanding four daily services to Zurich and seven to Geneva (three from Gatwick) which, together with one daily flight to Basle, adds up to half-a-million passengers a year between the two countries.

The two Austrian cities served are Vienna, the capital on the not-so-blue Danube, twice daily, and the Mozart city of Salzburg. The latter service is flown in conjunction with Austrian Airlines using McDonnell Douglas DC-9s. Salzburg is the access point to the country's most famous Alpine resorts.

The French Connection

The short hop across the Channel to France is among the oldest of the commercial airways in the world. Since the inauguration of the first-ever London-Paris service by Aircraft Transport and Travel on 25 August 1919, this prime route has always been fiercely contested and has invariably been flown by more than one UK airline. Today is no different and while British Airways is the principal carrier on the route with eight daily TriStar services between Heathrow Airport and Charles de Gaulle, Paris is also served six times daily from Gatwick and by Air UK from Stansted. Fitted out for 334 passengers in a two-class configuration, the British Airways TriStars carry a total of three-quarters of a million passengers a year between the two capitals, making it the most-travelled city pair in Europe. Scheduled flying time is one hour.

British Airways flies additionally to four other population centres, all numbered among the largest in France and, in their different ways, of great importance to the French economy. Daily nonstop Boeing 737 flights are operated to Lyon, a huge industrial area and centre of the textile industry in the southeast, and to Marseille, France's principal Mediterranean seaport. The 737 also provides four weekly services to Bordeaux, heart of the celebrated wine-growing region of Aquitaine along the Atlantic coast to the southwest. The twice-daily route to Nice, playground on the Cote d'Azur, is shared by the 757 and 737. As well as appealing to the leisure market, Nice is home to a sizeable engineering and chemical industry.

The English Channel is also the only short barrier which separates Britain and the Low Countries of Belgium and the Netherlands. Brussels and Amsterdam share the distinction with Paris of being part of a select group of cities which enjoyed the luxury of early air links in Europe, inauguration of flights from London having taken place in 1919 and 1920 respectively. Both have been served with little interruption ever since. British Airways presently flies six times a day from Heathrow and four times daily from Gatwick. Amsterdam also has a direct British Airways link with Birmingham. The once-a-day 737 flight to Luxembourg, the third of the Low Countries, is a much more recent addition.

The Iberian Peninsula

As the most favoured place in the sun for the British holiday maker, Spain in particular has seen an ever-increasing number of British Airways aircraft touch down at its airports. All these routes serve a mixture of business and leisure traffic, combining regular scheduled convenience with the freedom to 'go-as-you-please'.

Principal route is that to Madrid, the capital and business centre with two daily flights from Heathrow and one from Gatwick. Served once a day and twice respectively are Bilbao, the capital of the Basque region in the north, and Barcelona in the eastern province of Catalonia. Both are important commercial and industrial areas, the latter also giving access to the Costa Blanca, one of the world's most popular stretches of holiday coast. Two daily flights link Gatwick with Malaga, the Andalusian seashore town and gateway to the Costa del Sol.

British Airways flies to three cities in Portugal, the most western part of Europe, taking up a small strip of the peninsula on the Atlantic coast. Lisbon, the capital city which played such a vital role in BOAC's wartime aerial supply lines, is served daily from both London airports, while Oporto, Portugal's second city some 210 miles (340km) to the north and well known for its port-wine, has a three times a week connection from Gatwick. More frequent flights are operated to Faro in the south, heart of the Algarve and much loved by the English sunseeker.

One of the few remaining British outposts is Gibraltar, a rocky promontory jutting out from the southern tip of Spain, guarding the narrow entrance into the Mediterranean. The 'Rock' has had an air line with Britain since the early war years and British Airways currently flies five times a week from Gatwick, its late afternoon services alternating with those of GB Airways, the local airline in which British Airways, through British Airways Associated Companies, has a major stockholding. Both airlines use the Boeing 737 which is scheduled almost exclusively on the Iberian services. Only its higher-capacity sister aircraft, the Boeing 757, displaces it from the morning business flight to Madrid.

High Road to Scandinavia

In the immediate years before the outbreak of World War 2, British Airways, which was soon to join with Imperial Airways to form BOAC, began building up a weekly service between the British Isles and various Scandinavian countries. This was the only European air service from Britain, apart from that to Paris, to continue after war began, and was also one of the first routes to feel the impact of hostilities when war broke out between Finland and Russia. At that time this particular service terminated at Stockholm. Sweden was soon surrounded completely. As the only neutral country left in northern Europe, as well as being home to a substantial ball-bearing industry necessary to keep war machinery going, it was vital that communications were kept open. The 'ball-bearing' runs, flown from Scotland, were maintained under extremely difficult circumstances throughout the war, and were flown mostly at night and at high altitude, requiring oxygen for passengers and crew, to minimise the dangers from enemy fighters and anti-aircraft defences. British Airways planes to Scandinavia today fly even higher, but in open skies, and safety and comfort is a far cry from that experienced by some unfortunate people who had to make the wartime journey in the bomb bay of a twin-engined Mosquito.

Top right:
A British Airways Boeing 737 waiting to depart Budapest followed by a Tupolev Tu134 of Malév, the Hungarian national airline. *Péter Zsille*

Below:
One of several types scheduled on European Services, this BAC One-Eleven is rolled out of the paint shop in the new British Airways livery. *British Airways*

Bottom left:
One of Caledonian's 737-236s. *G. Dobson*

Bottom right:
Boeing 737-236 G-BKYH, shot at Tegel Airport, is one of six of the type based in Berlin. *Péter Zsille*

British Airways routes to Scandinavia serve primarily the business travel market, and all four countries have regular daily services from London. In Sweden, British Airways flies to the two largest cities, Stockholm the capital on the Baltic and Gothenburg, principal Scandinavian port on Sweden's west coast. Frequency on the Stockholm route is four times a day, while Gothenburg has one daily link. Other daily connections from London serve Helsinki, the Finnish capital and Stavanger, Norway's 'oil city', and there is sufficient traffic on the Oslo and Copenhagen services for three and four daily flights respectively. Copenhagen and Stockholm are the only Scandinavian destinations served from both London airports, all other flights operating from Heathrow alone. A mixture of Boeing 737s and 757s are scheduled on these routes, with the London-Gatwick-Copenhagen service flown with the new Airbus.

Services to Eastern Europe

Relations between Britain and the Eastern Bloc tend to suffer from cyclical uncertainties brought about by the marked difference in political ideology, but there have been signs over the last few years of a softening of attitude which, in the wake of 'Glasnost' is rapidly accelerating. As a result, British Airways business traffic has improved substantially in line with a general upsurge in trade. A still relatively small proportion of passengers travel on holiday, mainly to the Soviet Union and Hungary.

The Soviet Union is Britain's major trading partner in Eastern Europe, a fact which is reflected in daily services between London-Heathrow and Moscow's Sheremetievo 2 Airport. For the Western tourist, however, the city to visit is Leningrad, once seat of the Tsars and retaining many splendid buildings and treasures from those opulent times. British Airways serves the city once a week on Sunday with 737s.

Warsaw, the Polish capital, first served by the original British Airways in 1939, has daily flights in the summer, less out of season. Prague, capital of Czechoslovakia is served three times a week and the Danube city of Budapest in neighbouring Hungary daily. Both were first linked to London by Imperial Airways on a multi-stop route in April 1935.

British Airways scheduled destinations in Europe

While British Airways does not serve the German Democratic Republic on a year-round basis, a special daily passenger service for businessmen is operated twice a year to the week-long International Trade Fair in Leipzig, held annually in March and September. One-Elevens are scheduled at convenient times, early in the morning and around noon. Both Fairs exhibit consumer goods, with the Spring Fair additionally specialising in general and heavy engineering and electrical and electronics products. Textile machinery, chemicals, automotive industries and printing are features of the Autumn Fair.

Silver Blue Planes over the Mediterranean

British Airways aircraft are a familiar sight at many airports around the Mediterranean Sea. On the way, no less than seven points are served in Italy, headed by the capital Rome and the primary industrial and commercial centres of Milan, Genoa and Turin in the north of the country. Milan has five daily flights, followed by Rome with four and Turin with two, and Genoa once daily. Three to four weekly services to Bologna, Venice and Naples in response to tourism demands have been added from Gatwick in latter years, while business and cultural pursuits are the main reason for a daily service to Pisa/Florence, flown from Heathrow. Some 60 miles (100km) off the foot of Sicily lies Malta, a British possession prior to independence in 1964. Strong trade links tending towards tourism, provide the basis for two daily flights by British Airways from London-Gatwick. All flights are shared by the high-capacity Boeing 757 and Lockheed TriStar, and the A320.

Further to the east, the island of Cyprus has a recent history not unlike that of Malta, becoming an independent republic after a spell as a British Crown Colony. Britain still maintains a vital strategic air force base on the island, which supports a large services population and this, together with its attraction as a holiday hot spot, gives rise to substantial traffic between London and Larnaca, served by several British Airways flights a day during the summer.

Istanbul, on the European side of Turkey, has a twice daily service and Tel-Aviv, the Israeli capital, is served at a lesser frequency. Of increasing importance, both from a business and tourist point of view, is Athens, the ancient Greek capital on the Aegean. 737s and TriStars are employed twice daily on this high-density route from London-Heathrow and there is a weekend 757 flight from Gatwick.

British Airways Berlin

Berlin, or more accurately West Berlin, is a unique western exclave in the heart of the German Democratic Republic, separated from the eastern sector of the city by the infamous wall erected in August 1961. Internal German Services (IGS) are wholly dependent on this oddly

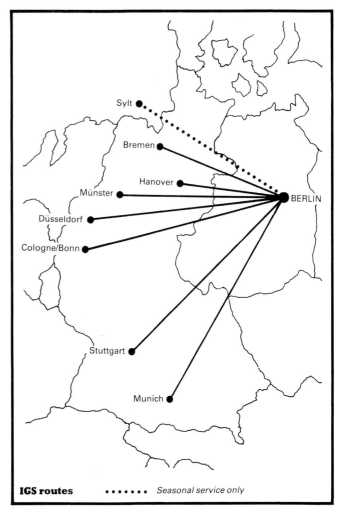

IGS routes •••••• *Seasonal service only*

contrived political situation which prohibits German airlines from serving Berlin but allows the victorious nations, even 40 years after the end of the war, exclusive access to its air transport needs. Regulation is in the hands of three Allied Civil Air Attachés resident in Bonn, who are briefed by their home governments but also consult with the Federal Government and the Berlin Senate, although there is no legal requirement to do so. This contact applies particularly to the fixing of tariffs, approval of schedules and other related matters. In recognition of their special status, all services into and out of West Berlin are subject to a subsidy, granted by the Federal Authorities, reducing the fare paid by each passenger by as much as 17% on the Hannover route and 14% on the longer services.

Since the signing of a far-reaching transit agreement between East and West Germany in 1971/72, traffic of all modes of transport has almost doubled from the 14 million then travelling between Berlin and the West and is continuing its upward trend. In sharp contrast, this same agreement switched traffic from air to surface, resulting in a sharp decline in air transport. This has settled at around 19% of the total volume and is now showing signs of a slight upturn.

The British Airways market share is at present some 34% of the IGS traffic with Pan American the main competitor, serving Frankfurt, Hamburg, Nuremberg,

Right:
A total of twelve twin-turboprop BAe 748s — nicknamed 'The Budgie' — are in service with Highlands Division. In addition to 44 passengers, there is plenty of room for baggage, newspapers, mail and freight. *British Airways/Adrian Meredith*

Below:
BAe 748s supplement the existing Boeing 737 fleet on some of the less dense routes of the Internal German Services (IGS). *Péter Zsille*

Bottom:
The first of eight BAe ATPs ordered by British Airways for use by its Highlands Division. All eight aircraft will be in service for the 1989 summer season. *BAe*

Above:
Illustrating the two principal activities of British Airways Helicopters (and BEA Helicopters before) is the Sikorsky S-61N Mk 2 photographed at St Mary's on the scheduled passenger service between Cornwall and the Scilly Isles and . . .

Below:
. . . at Aberdeen on North Sea oil and gas support flights. The new British Airways markings were applied for only a short time prior to the company's sale in September 1986 to British International Helicopters Ltd. *Austin J Brown*

Above:
Concorde looks in at Turin-Caselle, the northern Italian commercial and industrial centre, normally served four times a week with Boeing 737s.
SAGAT

Stuttgart and Munich. Air France, the other major airline of the Allied powers, flies three times a day from Berlin to Düsseldorf and Paris. Three regional airlines from the UK and the United States complete the current picture, with Dan-Air flying between Berlin and Saarbrücken, Berlin European to Friedrichshaven and Copenhagen, and Tempelhof Airways from Berlin to Dortmund and Paderborn. The British Airways share is at present equivalent to 1.25 million passengers a year of which almost two-thirds travel on business and include a high percentage of frequent flyers. This passenger total is generated by the eight-point scheduled services network which links Berlin with Bremen, Cologne/Bonn, Düsseldorf, Hannover, Münster/Osnabrück, Stuttgart, Munich and Sylt, together with a comprehensive charter programme to the main holiday destinations along the Mediterranean. All services are operated with a mixed fleet of advanced Boeing 737-236s and HS 748s producing healthy average load factors of 62%, leaving enough reserves for possible future growth. Since 1 September 1946 when a BEA Dakota first landed in Berlin, British Airways has carried in excess of 32 million passengers on its services to and from the city.

With heavy competition on the major routes, mainly from Pan American, opportunities for future expansion appear to be limited to the inclusion of a few smaller cities on the longer routes. There is also presently much talk about north-south connections via Berlin, such as Scandinavia-Berlin-Austria or similar routes. These are, however, mere flights of fancy: it is difficult to perceive the governments at the ends of such a route granting traffic rights to a third country carrier.

The Berlin market distinguishes Germany from all other countries served by British Airways. It supports the overall performance of the airline by adding to revenue and operating surplus, sufficient to cover interest charges and aircraft replacement and by improving the punctuality average which, on the IGS, is considerably better at 97% than elsewhere on the system. This is partly the result of introducing the 737, which is fitted with a Category III blind landing system which permits a vertical decision height of only 15m and a runway visual length of 250m. Other market features are an extremely high percentage (96%) of German sales and price-sensitivity to the threat posed by surface competition, especially to the non-business segment.

It is a fact, albeit somewhat surprising, that 80% of all passengers live in the Federal Republic which appears to show that Berliners are clearly less reticent than their West German compatriots in using the motorcar to drive through the GDR. British Airways actively promotes the city as a business and cultural centre through its 'Golden Conference Table' programme which has now been running since 1976 and special fly-drive short-stay holiday packages for families in conjunction with Avis and leading hotels such as the Berlin Intercontinental.

Since the retirement of the Super One-Elevens in March 1986, the fleet currently based in Berlin comprises 106-seat Boeing 737-236 Advanced twin-jets and 44-seat HS 748 turboprop aircraft. A technical base is also maintained at Tegel Airport which undertakes routine maintenance and the 'Deep Clean' operation of the entire 737 fleet. This set-up makes British Airways an important employer with more than half of the 800 personnel on strength in Germany including the 130 cabin staff, based in Berlin. The operation is staffed overwhelmingly by German nationals with less than two dozen British subjects on the books.

The special status of this divided city is likely to remain on the political map of Central Europe for many decades to come but the liberalisation of air transport within the European community due to come into effect in 1992 will not bypass Berlin. Already the US mega carriers have put in a plethora of route applications to serve almost every sizeable city in Germany and those of neighbouring countries from Berlin and two, American Airlines and TWA have recently been given approval by the US part of the Allied Air Directorate. The deregulation lobby is powerful and gaining momentum and competition will be fierce. British Airways, with its strong base, is ready to meet the challenge.

7 British Airways Cargo – Tonnes of Trade

British Airways is today the world's seventh largest cargo carrier. This dramatic achievement has been made possible through the establishment, in 1983, of British Airways Cargo as a separate business centre in recognition of the vital importance of revenue produced by cargo from what would otherwise be grossly under-utilised or even empty space. Prior to that, cargo was viewed as little more than a by-product of the airline's passenger services but growth has been such that the revenue, now approaching £300 million a year, has become a critical factor in the financial viability of the airline, especially on long-haul routes. British Airways Cargo employs a total of 2,000 people, of whom 1,200 are based in the UK. Headquarters is the World Cargocentre at London-Heathrow and there are other major cargo establishments at Gatwick, Manchester, Birmingham and Glasgow Airports.

British Airways' extensive global network of routes, incorporating 165 prime destinations from London, has given the airline a distinct advantage to make full use of the tremendous opportunities for expansion of its cargo business. According to British Airways Cargo Managing Director Geoff Bridges, the key to its success to date – and in the future – lies in developing and pursuing robust strategies and being able to offer a service which is firmly founded on three important qualities: integrity, speed and simplicity, in that order.

Strategies are based on optimising, wherever possible, the traffic mix on scheduled services by maximising returns from traditional cargo; progressively enhancing the passenger product and a step-by-step move into the premium cargo and still fast-expanding courier and express markets, in the process developing London as the new prime international cargo hub. In addition, British Airways is continually widening its network with new interline agreements, capacity purchase and building up air/sea interfaces and ground distribution systems. Comprehensive trucking in the UK in combination with new hubs, opened in Maastricht, Helsinborg and Lyon , has enabled British Airways to considerably strengthen its base market to encompass the whole of Europe. This now accounts for just over 50% of the total business, divided in near equal portions between the UK and continental Europe and Scandinavia. Trucking is necessary because the majority of European flights are operated with narrow-bodied aircraft which do not have the cargo capacity to meet consumer demands.

The next largest market area is the USA, Canada and the Caribbean with 20%, and British Airways is determined to achieve increased market penetration through pioneering a nationwide trucking network from its 18 US gateways which will enable it to offer next-day delivery from the UK to virtually anywhere in America. There are other advances, not least in air/sea traffic across the Pacific into the US west coast gateways; the further development of Miami as a gateway city with the new South American services feeding in produce from Caracas and flowers out of Bogota; and Speedbird Express, British Airways' door-to-door package service. Nearly three-quarters of all US revenue is generated overseas and more than half of all cargo is trans-shipped through London.

Cargo traffic continues to grow at a faster pace than that of passengers, due primarily to heightened customer expectation. This is particularly evident with regard to perishable fruit and vegetables from all over the world which are now on sale in supermarkets all the year round. India and parts of Africa and South America are all improving fast as originating markets for products of the soil and there is no slowing down of growth from the

Engineering Excellence — 1

Top right:
Aircraft emergency chutes and inflatable dinghies are only two of many items which have to be maintained to a very high standard by Technical Services. *British Airways*

Centre right:
Ground Simulator training has been developed to demonstrate and practise a huge range of aircraft maintenance tasks. *British Airways*

Bottom right:
Maintenance of Concorde is a complicated procedure, requiring particular attention and increased effort. *British Airways/Adrian Meredith*

Far right, top:
TriStar 500 G-BLUS sits in the hangar for a major maintenance check. *British Airways/Adrian Meredith*

Far right, bottom:
A Boeing 737 completely surrounded by gantries and platforms undergoes a major 'P' check at Heathrow. *British Airways/Adrian Meredith*

Above:
Capacity Optimisation Manager Bernie Knill with the next revolution – the lighter and stronger see-through cargo container.
British Airways/Adrian Meredith

traditionally cheap, labour-intensive manufacturing centres of the Far East, specialising in textiles and electronic goods.

At present nearly 20% of British Airways Cargo earnings come from the top end of the market and this is expected to increase steadily, eventually overtaking traditional business in revenue terms. To take account of this clear trend, British Airways has instituted a capacity control system which ensures space is always available for high-yield items. An Express Handling Unit has been established at Heathrow to be progressively expanded to other stations worldwide as will Speedbird Express. Courier check-in facilities at Heathrow and same-day domestic parcel services, both organised as joint ventures, are also in hand.

Passenger product improvements include the popular accompanied pets scheme, and the new 'Luggage Line' unaccompanied baggage service where passengers can choose a number of different options, from airport-to-airport to door-to-door delivery. New services for importers are 'Clearway', a comprehensive import brokerage facility at Heathrow Airport, and a business introduction service designed to offer a consultancy advising on packaging, market potential, costs and likely returns on specific commodities. British Airways is casting its net

wide to encompass all aspects of the cargo world, and the fact that a high percentage of revenue comes from repeat business, shows that the airline is on the right track.

Passenger Planes Tops in Cargo

British Airways carries more traffic, currently over 250,000 tonnes per annum in the bellyhold of passenger aircraft, than it did a few years ago when operating dedicated all-cargo aircraft. By designing new hull-hugging pallets and containers – the latest in lighter see-through polycarbonate – and altering the hold configuration of its TriStars, cargo capacity on British Airways passenger fleet has been boosted by 30%. This is the equivalent of adding two Boeing 747F Freighters to the fleet, but at significantly lower cost.

Some 90% of the total tonnage is carried by the long range TriStars which have a cargo capacity of 11 tonnes, and Boeing 747 fleets, the latter including six 747-200Bs in combi configuration. These versatile aircraft can uplift 40 tonnes of cargo in addition to the airline's standard complement of up to 220 passengers. With almost any number of passenger/cargo variations possible, the Combi is the vehicle best suited to meet the airline's often unpredictable requirements in the ever-changing markets of the future. To ensure maximum flexibility, British Airways is looking towards a position whereby between a quarter and a third of the 747 fleet will be Combis, with up to six of these aircraft permanently configured in a dual passenger/cargo upperdeck layout. The Combis have done much to boost profits and more aircraft will further enhance the product by increasing both scheduled coverage and nonstop capability. This will become increasingly important with the introduction of the larger extended-range Boeing 747-400s beginning at the end of the decade. British Airways is already investigating how to get maximum cargo capacity from the 400 Series, 19 of which are on order as part of the latest fleet update, and it is hoped that through relocating and miniaturising equipment, an extra 20cu m of space could be provided. Fibre optics control systems, taking up less room may also free additional space for possible use of cargo. The 747-400 will give British Airways the opportunity to fly nonstop across its whole network with the exception of Europe/Australia, though even this may be possible by the turn of the century with prop-fan powered aircraft like the proposed 747-500.

Whilst wide-bodied aircraft are clearly best suited to carrying traditional volumetric cargo, the airline has also experimented with the narrow-bodied Boeing 757, by testing a new aircraft with a Boeing-designed mini container system in one hold. This is undergoing further development and if it proves successful, could add a new dimension to the short-haul freight market.

Smaller amounts of freight are also carried on the other short-range aircraft in the fleet including the BAC One-Eleven, Boeing 737-236 and HS 748, as well as Concorde, which gives British Airways the capability to offer a same-day service to the USA for high-priority packages.

Speedbird Express

Speedbird Express is the British Airways all-inclusive door-to-door package service. Since its introduction in 1982 with a single service to Germany, Speedbird has expanded at an annual growth rate of 50% and the network now stretches right across the globe encompassing 38 countries. In addition to the UK and most European countries, the service reaches out to the USA, South Africa, Kenya, Malawi, Bahrain, Qatar, the United Arab Emirates, Oman, Singapore, Hong Kong, Japan and Australia, with Mauritius, the Caribbean, South America, New Zealand and parts of South-East Asia planned to be next. A reciprocal import service is currently available from 20 countries.

Work is nearing completion on a £400,000 complex at Heathrow's World Cargocentre to provide Speedbird and the closely-allied Express Handling Unit with additional warehousing and office accommodation to take account of the expected increase in business. Experts are generally agreed that by 1995, world-wide door-to-door revenues could be as high as £18 billion. Speedbird wants a slice of the action and is set fair to get it.

The Speedbird Express system provides for collection, export documentation, carriage, customs clearance and delivery to final address, all at an inclusive price, and guarantees despatch no later than the day after collection, if not on the same day. There is no limit on consignment size or number of pieces, although each package must contain only one type of commodity. Certain items such as livestock, perishable foodstuffs, personal effects and other specifics are not acceptable for carriage by this service, which relies strongly on speedy customs clearance. Every consignment is shipped direct with its own Airwaybill and can be traced at any stage of the journey by the British Airways computer.

One of Speedbird's greatest assets is Concorde which, as mentioned previously, can offer a same-day service to the USA. A package collected in central London at 8 o'clock in the morning, will be delivered in downtown Manhattan, New York by late afternoon. Altogether, deliveries can be made to any of over 20,000 points in the USA including Alaska, Hawaii and Puerto Rico, with all urgent shipments travelling by Concorde for distribution from New York.

The British Airways Express Handling Unit provides rapid handling for small, high-premium freight, airport to airport and although working closely with Speedbird Express, has its own dedicated staff and airside vehicle fleet. The Unit is able to handle urgent shipments up to 100kg in weight of such items as documents, samples, spares or anything where speed is of the essence. Consignments can be accepted up to 45min before scheduled flight departure time, with no need to book in advance. On the import side, shipments are available for presentation to Customs 45min after arrival. Clearance normally takes another similar period. Transhipment anywhere within the British Airways route system is available within two hours of touchdown. One-third of the Unit's throughput comes from Speedbird Express.

The Flying Pets Club

For a nation of animal lovers such as the British – widely recognised as such throughout the world – the innovative British Airways Flying Pets Club which enables domestic cats and dogs to travel as excess baggage on the same aircraft as their owners, has gone a long way towards taking the inevitable stress out of flying for both pets and owners.

Until the scheme was introduced into British Airways by Cargo Business Manager Geoff Birchall in the summer of 1985, initially covering Europe and later extended to other parts of the world, owners had to take their pets to the Heathrow Cargocentre at least four hours before take-off for booking in as conventional cargo. There was also no guarantee that they would travel on the same aircraft as their owners. The whole procedure was time-consuming and inconvenient. Now on the day of departure, the passenger can take the pet to the passenger check-in desk, pay its fare and see it safely into its travelling box which can be supplied at nominal cost. The pet is then loaded into a warm aircraft hold, and all stations en route are signalled to check the animal's well-being, and water it if necessary. At the final destination the passenger collects his pet and, providing documents are in order, it is cleared through customs with the ordinary baggage. In addition to a special passport (issued to every pet and to contain care and handling instructions, flight details and destination) a certificate of good health and one for rabies

Terminal 4

Right:
The 2,000ft-long departure concourse in Heathrow's Terminal 4 contains 64 British Airways check-in desks.
British Airways/Adrian Meredith

Below:
Passengers await their British Airways flight to the other side of the world in the comfort of the Terminal 4 departure lounge.
British Airways/Adrian Meredith

Left:
The Roland Klein uniforms for 15,000 customer contact staff complement the new look of the airline.
British Airways/Adrian Meredith

Bottom left:
A smart new appearance and greater allegiance to its motto has already paid British Airways handsome dividends.
British Airways/Adrian Meredith

Bottom right:
From the House of André Peters the new workwear features the smart grey and red Speedwing, the principal element of the overall corporate design.
British Airways/Adrian Meredith

is usually sufficient. The fare is in many instances cheaper than sending animals by normal cargo service, but as a general rule works out at 1% per kg of the first class passenger fare, the same as excess baggage.

For the vast majority of British Airways destinations, these procedures present no undue difficulties. There are, however, some notable exceptions including the UK, Ireland, Australia, New Zealand, South Africa, Cyprus, Hong Kong and the Seychelles, which operate strict quarantine regulations requiring all animals to arrive as cargo.

Outbound traffic presently amounts to 4,000 pets a year, with around 1,800 inbound, bringing in an annual revenue exceeding £4 million. Half of the total traffic in both directions is between Britain and the USA with the remaining half divided in roughly equal proportions between the UK and countries with large expatriate working and Services populations such as Bahrain, Canada, Germany, Kuwait, the United Arab Emirates, Zimbabwe and Zambia.

Another service introduced recently provides facilities at Heathrow for pets in transit. In the event of the time between connecting flights exceeding four hours, pets are taken to the quarantine centre to be cared for, fed and watered.

A 'petscort' system is also offered where a pet is collected, accompanied throughout the journey by qualified kennel staff, and delivered right to the door at its destination. Although by its very nature quite expensive, it is yet another addition to British Airways' constantly improving customer product, and around four pet owners avail themselves of this special service each month.

It is not only pets that get special treatment from British Airways Cargo, horses too get an easier ride. The airline owns two specially-designed horseboxes which can accommodate three horses at a time and is completely enclosed, thus protecting the occupants against the weather. There is a seat for a groom and the box can be easily cleaned out, making it suitable for carrying general cargo when not required for horses.

Carrying livestock is a growing business for the airline, and while domestic cats and dogs and valuable race-horses make up the great majority of the total volume of traffic, British Airways handles on a regular basis many unusual and exotic specimens from the animal kingdom. As with human passengers, these are also treated with care.

Cargocentres Across Country

The vital importance to the country's economy of the North of England, which covers half the entire UK manufacturing industry, has been the basis for the rapid growth of cargo traffic at Manchester and British Airways' firm commitment to the region, founded on the establishment of the most up-to-date cargo facility in the UK. Built at a cost of nearly £3.5 million, the highly-mechanised Northern cargo terminal is located at the heart of Manchester International Airport's custom-built complex, developing rapidly as a cargo

community. Most large forwarders are now well-established and with major motorways converging from the North, the Midlands and the South of England, and the air routes of British Airways linking Manchester with most important European cities and other world markets, it is a convenient place to do business. With 75 domestic Shuttle flights a week to London and direct flights to Aberdeen, Belfast, Bristol, Glasgow and Jersey, other UK market centres can also be reached on a daily basis.

The Manchester Cargocentre currently handles more than 15,000 tonnes of freight per year with another similar tonnage for other airlines serviced by British Airways, including Austrian Airlines, Iberia, KLM, Manx Airlines, Pan American, Sabena, SAS, Singapore Airlines and Swissair. This is still some way short of the airport's total capacity of 50,000 tonnes, but this is expected to be taken up soon as new scheduled services are being added and an increasing number of airlines come to Manchester.

The Cargocentre has been sited to provide good access and the building itself has been designed to make cargo handling as easy as possible. On the eastern side there is a road services park for exclusive use of British

Below:
The Northern Cargocentre at Manchester is the most advanced cargo terminal in the UK with the emphasis on mechanical and computer control.
British Airways Cargo

Bottom:
Huge cargo containers sit side by side in the cavernous aircraft hold.
British Airways Cargo

Airways, which can take the largest lorries currently in use. Two hydraulically-operated truck-doors and dock-levellers ensure that cargo can be loaded and unloaded from any comfortable height. On the opposite side, three doors are equipped with fast acting automatic canvas screens which are activated by vehicle positioning in or out of the warehouse, and help to maintain a balanced temperature. Each of these doors is linked to 20-tonne capacity weighbridges and there are two further doors for outsize cargo. A major feature of the centre is the narrow isle storage system which has 900 positions and storage for 33 winged pallets. Container handling is simplified by the Elevating Transport Vehicle – or ETV – which weighs, handles, stores and unloads units for up to six full flights at a time. There are also four pallet-building positions, two of which can be recessed into the floor and equipped with weighscales. Other special facilities include the only quarantine rooms at Manchester Airport, radioactive storage area, a strongroom for valuable and precious cargo, and a small freezer unit for holding perishable foodstuffs and sensitive medical supplies. A warm room provides a constant temperature environment for consignments of birds, tropical fish and other delicate livestock.

More than 100 British Airways staff operate the Cargocentre on a 7-days-a-week, 24-hour basis, providing comprehensive services to meet all export, import, transhipment and domestic demands. All the operations are centralised in the same building which makes for better efficiency. As at Heathrow, the BA80 computer provides an instantaneous documentation system for flight control, load assembly, tracing and accounting and gives complete access to all British Airways flight operations, such as passenger loads and reservations, on all UK and overseas stations. The system is further enhanced with the use of mobile VDU units based on the British Telecom 2000 system, which enables warehouse staff to access the BA80 without the need to use an office-based computer terminal.

Efficiency and customer service are always in the forefront and British Airways' close-out time – the latest that export cargo can be accepted prior to the flight departure – has been whittled down to only 75min. For Datapost it is a mere 30min, and even this is negotiable. For incoming cargo, British Airways strives to have documentation available within half-an-hour and the consignment ready for clearance inside two hours. Collection and cartage can be arranged anywhere in the North of England and the service also includes the raising of export clearance documents and community transit forms for EEC destinations, progress reports and proof of delivery.

The Gatwick Cargocentre, with an annual throughput of 130,000 tonnes of freight and 13,000 tonnes of mail, is one of the busiest in the UK and second only to Heathrow. A new mechanical handling system has been installed which allows more efficient movement of freight and will facilitate further growth. Market interface with British Airways' domestic and overseas destinations is provided by twice-daily truck services between the two

London airports. Regular trucks also link Gatwick direct with Birmingham, Wales, Scotland, Northern Ireland and the Channel Islands. As well as meeting the demands of its own schedules, British Airways also handles several international carriers at Gatwick, including Air Zimbabwe, CAAC, Cameroon Airlines, Gibraltar Airways, Jersey European Airways and the extensive freighter operations of Philippine Airlines, Cathay Pacific and the Royal Canadian Air Force.

The latest cargocentre to be completely updated is the **Cargocentre Midlands**, officially opened on 10 December 1986. Built at Birmingham's New International Airport, it comprises under one roof almost 52,000sq ft (5,000sq m) of warehouse and office space for the exclusive use of British Airways and HM Customs. Like the airline's other facilities, it boasts the latest mechanical handling and computer control systems. Birmingham, home to England's only inland freeport and the National Exhibition Centre, serves the industrial heartland of the UK, with a growing list of direct flights to London, Scotland, Northern Ireland, the North and East Midlands, as well as to major cities in France, Germany, Spain, Cyprus, the Netherlands and the Irish Republic. There are also regular truck services to and from Heathrow and Manchester.

Maastricht – Cargo Crossroads of Europe

In April 1986, British Airways established a major Western European trucking hub to support its long-haul cargo operations. Although British Airways was by no means the first airline to venture into road trucking, it led the way in creating such an important hub outside its home country. On first impression, Maastricht appears an odd choice to serve British Airways, but closer inspection reveals all. The city's advantages lie in its location in the extreme southeast of the Netherlands, sharing a long border with the heavily-industrialised Ruhr region of West Germany, as well as the Belgian provinces of Liège and Limburg, in the heart of a 50 million consumer catchment area within a 250km radius. It is also linked to a most efficient rail, road and waterway system, giving easy access to the whole of Europe.

Maastricht boasts extensive modern office premises and bonded warehousing with a 24-hour customs service. The airport's cargo facilities were first opened in 1979 and subsequent extensions have increased the annual capacity to 70,000 tonnes. Since British Airways moved in, traffic has been boosted now to exceed 50,000 tonnes throughput a year.

The £1 million British Airways cargo terminal was commissioned for the airline by the Maastricht Airport Authority, and constructed by local builders in record time, taking less than five months from conception in late February 1986 to the official opening in mid-July. From April and throughout the remaining construction period, British Airways used temporary facilities to put the hub into operation. The cargo terminal, incorporating 2,000sq m of offices and warehousing, has an outside asphalt hard-

Concorde —
The Jewel in the Crown

Left:
Concorde cuts the Atlantic crossing to 3½hr, serving the US cities of New York, Washington and Miami.
British Airways/Adrian Meredith

Right:
A slender thoroughbred: Concorde at Heathrow's Terminal 4. *Arthur Kemsley*

Left:
The star attraction wherever it makes an appearance — Concorde at Budapest Ferihegy Airport, Hungary, in 1986.
Péter Zsille

Below:
The massive Rolls-Royce/SNECMA Olympus turbojets drive Concorde to twice the speed of sound.
British Airways/Adrian Meredith

standing area for trucks, and is equipped with seven overhead opening doors, two pallet-building stations and an automatic storage and retrieval system. In order to create an unrestricted operating area, the roof is supported by large-span beams of laminated Swedish pine.

The Maastricht hub enables British Airways to handle more cargo through London to connect with its worldwide network and speeds the flow of traffic both to and from Europe. This also means more frequent collections and deliveries, shorter transhipment times through Heathrow and a wider coverage of Europe. At any one time, up to 20 vehicles can be on the road for British Airways. Small, high-priority consignments continue to go by air.

Freight travels by road to Maastricht where it is loaded onto high-frequency road trains to Heathrow or Manchester. At present, West Germany, France, the Benelux countries, Italy, Spain, Portugal, Greece, Turkey and Scandinavia are all linked into the Maastricht hub, and new European countries will be added as the market develops. The continental road trucking has been contracted out, but within the UK British Airways runs its own trucks which cover the main regional airports, as well as off-line points like Humberside, Luton, Norwich and East Midlands. Cargo to Maastricht from the UK goes either via Heathrow, or on a special six-times-a-week service, linking it with Manchester through Birmingham and Gatwick.

Below:
Comprehensive trucking in the UK in combination with its Maastricht hub has enabled British Airways to strengthen its market base to encompass the whole of Europe.
British Airways Cargo

All paperwork is prepared at Maastricht and BA80 computers, identical to those installed at the Heathrow Cargocentre, provide all necessary details of each consignment, such as Airwaybills and a breakdown of cargo in each container. This information is used by London to issue loading instructions and flight allocation, without the need to physically break down a shipment and rebuild it.

In its first year, British Airways Maastricht handled on average about 1,400 tonnes of cargo a month originating on the continent, with a similar amount of business destined for Europe. To British Airways, this annual total of 30,000 tonnes was worth more than £20 million – but this was only the beginning.

Route through the World Cargocentre

The World Cargocentre at Heathrow Airport handles more than 12,000 cargo consignments a week on over 250 daily flights, both inbound and outbound. This adds up to almost 200,000 tonnes of freight passing through the Cargocentre in a year, comprising imports, exports and domestic and international transhipments, all made possible through the application of high-technology handling and comprehensive computer control.

A requirement to ship by air begins with a call to Skyload, the British Airways Cargo reservation system, staffed round the clock by experienced personnel who will advise on every aspect of exporting by air, including documentation, acceptability, packing and rates. With direct access on the BA80 computer to the latest flight and load situations, availability of space to any of British Airways' worldwide destinations can be instantly confirmed. A booking can be made up to 14 days in advance of the flight and once this has been accepted, the

consignment can be delivered in person to the Cargo-centre or alternatively, be collected by a British Airways-approved freight forwarding agent, of which there are some 150 covering the London area alone. After the relevant documents have been checked and cleared at the Customs Reception Lounge, consignment and papers are taken to the Cargo Reception where a further double check ensures that both are in order. An Airwaybill number is allocated and all applicable data, such as flight, destination and size, weight and volume, are entered on the BA80 computer and updated at every step along the parcel's journey. The Airwaybill number is unique to every consignment; without it the consignment would be difficult to trace or effect customs clearance. Delivery to Cargo Reception can be made up to between four and six hours prior to flight departure.

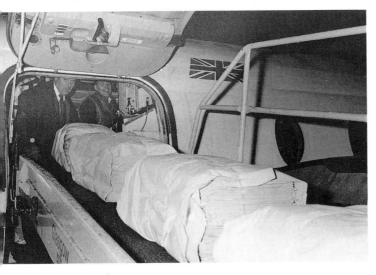

Above:
Mail and small freight on board the 748s in the Highlands and islands of Scotland may not register the massive tonnages of the Jumbos, but is a vital element of British Airways services to outlying communities.
British Airways/PR Consultants Scotland

In recent years, following the spread of terrorism across the world, security has taken on a higher priority and cargoes bound for certain destinations and/or on specific flights are screened before their entry into the export cargo holding area. Screening is undertaken by means of X-ray facilities similar to those found in passenger terminals, supervised by very experienced British Airways staff with a Service or Police background, who make a major contribution to Heathrow's reputation for being among the world's most secure airports.

In the holding area, cargo is allocated to designated bays for long-haul, short-haul Concorde flights, or to special locations permanently set aside for goods of an unusual nature. At Heathrow, these include cold stores for frozen goods or delicate medical specimens, livestock rooms, a radioactive room for medical isotopes, mortuary and stores for vulnerable and valuable items. There are also special racks for press materials, urgent aircraft spares and diplomatic cargo.

In the meantime, a load list is prepared by the Capacity Control Unit (CapCon) which takes into account the exact weight and cubic space of each piece of cargo, and determines the best onboard weight distribution for optimum flight performance. Assessing accurately the volume of each of the millions of cargo packages dealt with each year in order to make best use of space and maximising revenue, has been a perennial problem,. until British Airways got together with Integrated Photomatrix (PIL) to develop V-Scan. The equipment accepts a sequence of single packages of any shape, weighing between 0.5kg and 450kg, which are transferred direct from forklift truck onto the loading conveyor, weighscale platform and through the volumetric scanner. Passing at a uniform speed of 20m/min, opto-electronic scanning acquires a complete profile of each item and once the expected total number for the shipment has been received, the machine prints a ticket containing full weight and volume information of the complete consignment. CapCon thus manages the loading operation 'on paper' and is ultimately responsible for the final flight manifest. Manifesting begins about 18hrs before departure.

When all planning has been completed with the issuing of the flight control checklist, cargo handlers locate and pick up all the freight for a specific flight and load it into containers or loose-fill pallets, depending on the type of aircraft scheduled. The ETV (Elevating Transport Vehicle), a key feature in the efficient container handling in both import and export halls, then weighs, stacks and stores containers mechanically until the flight is called. At that time, the ETV unloads containers into trucks waiting airside for transportation to the waiting aircraft.

Import cargo accounts for 74,000 tonnes of the total tonnage with transhipments contributing another 56,000 tonnes. All import consignments are brought to the Cargocentre where details of each are keyed into the BA80 computer as they come off the aircraft. Customs entries are then passed to HM Customs, located in the same building, enabling British Airways to offer a faster and much more efficient service. When the shipment has cleared customs, the BA80 prints a release note authorising collection. This usually takes 6-8hrs from the time the aircraft is unloaded. Additionally, the World Cargocentre is linked to HM Customs ACP computer network for import inventory and clearances, and to its own ICES computerised accounting system which can produce immediate invoice information.

At the World Cargocentre, British Airways also provides cargo handling services for a number of other airlines. In the majority of cases this service includes export, import and reservations facilities. The airlines are Cyprus Airways, Brymon Airways, Ethiopian Airlines, Ghana Airways, LOT Polish Airlines, Balkan Bulgarian Airlines, Malev Hungarian Airlines, CSA Czechoslovak Airlines, Air Mauritius, Tarom Romanian Airlines, South African Airways, Sudan Airways and Aeroflot Soviet Airlines.

Boeing 747 — Size of an Elephant

Right:
Flying high: Boeing 747 *City of Durham* outward bound.
British Airways/Adrian Meredith

Below:
The enormous size of the Jumbo is evident when compared with these airport service vehicles.

Bottom left:
As is to be expected, the huge 747 offers an attractive wide-body interior with plenty of legroom.
British Airways/Adrian Meredith

Bottom right:
Cabin staff undergo thorough training for their demanding task before joining their colleagues on board, seen here inside a 747.

Right:
In addition to 366 passengers, the Boeing 747-136 can also carry cargo.
British Airways/Adrian Meredith

8 British Airways – Engineering Excellence

It is a well-established fact that most airline passengers show little interest in the state of serviceability of the airframe or the engines that drive them through the sky. Despite a growing awareness and knowledge about the aircraft they may be flying in, passengers are mostly quite content to take the professional integrity and engineering competence of British Airways for granted. What they are generally looking for is an efficient and friendly cabin service, a clean and comfortable aircraft and a punctual operation. The punctual despatch of flights, however, relies on the availability of serviceable aircraft and at Heathrow and Gatwick together with some 165 line stations throughout the world, British Airways has comprehensive engineering facilities to ensure that aircraft are available at all times to meet its vast operational requirements.

Services at Heathrow Engineering Base, spread over an area of 220 acres (890,000sq m) comprise routine minor and major maintenance checks and defect rectification, major modifications, refurbishment of cabin interiors, component changes, stripping/painting and cleaning of aircraft, as well as major structural repairs. Off-base services include defect rectification, unit changes and aircraft structural and major on-site repair work.

Backup is provided by Production Engineering which takes care of planning and co-ordinating each individual input and development of maintenance and overhaul programmes, Avionic and General Workshops and Technical Services. Avionics Workshops provide in-house re-certification, repair, overhaul, test and modification of aircraft components and systems. Complex avionics are processed by Automatic Test Equipment (ATE) ensuring greater service speed and accuracy.

General Workshops support the aircraft operation by providing overhaul and repair of a wide range of aircraft parts and components, together with serviceable stocks to agreed levels. The large range of parts, components and assemblies maintained, covers aircraft mechanical pneumatic and hydraulic systems, including life-controlled and 'on condition' items. Extensive Technical Services include the provision and control of aircraft and aircraft equipment evaluation, aircraft performance, technical performance and development of aircraft and aircraft equipment, quality control, development and planning of aircraft and accessory modifications and control of preparation, standards and distribution of technical publications.

The Gatwick engineering and maintenance facilities, greatly enhanced with the acquisition of British Caledonian, employs a staff approaching 1500. Apart from fleet maintenance of Gatwick-based aircraft, third party work remains an important element.

The Cost of Engineering

Over recent years, demands on Engineering have increased considerably and this has been reflected in a proportionate rise in costs. However, a greater emphasis on planning and consequently more efficient working practices have seen to it that an annual growth of 5% in workload has not also resulted in correspondingly higher manpower levels. Engineering expenditure amounts to £300 million a year, but some £50 million is being recovered by undertaking third party work for other customers. A significant proportion of this comes from engine overhaul contracts in South Wales, but sizeable contributions are additionally received from aircraft maintenance and component overhaul, aircraft repair, station handling and various training schemes. A charge is also made to Caledonian Airways for engineering work carried out on aircraft operated by that subsidiary company.

By far the largest single item cost relates to staff pay, pensions and insurance, making up a massive £100 million plus, or one-third of total expenditure. Technical materials consumption eats up another £100 million. Approximately 50% of this is incurred at the Engine Overhaul facility at Nantgarw, and by aircraft type half of the total is needed for Boeing 747 aircraft and engines. Each 747 consumes on average £2.5 million worth of materials per year, Concorde just over £1.5 million and the TriStar around £1 million. The short-haul Boeing 737 and BAC One-Eleven are significantly less voracious, as is the newer Boeing 757. The annual average cost of materials across the whole fleet amounts to £250 for each flying hour.

The other principal costs are made up from standing charges, such as amortisation of aircraft and technical spares holdings, subcontract work, and from materials used for modification programmes.

'TIME' to Spares

On 25/26 April 1987, British Airways Engineering completed a major transformation of its working practices, when it switched to its new TIME (Total Inventory Management for Engineering) System, created to introduce a much tighter control of the airline's several million engineering parts. TIME was developed to effectively combine its previous Joint Stock and Drive systems, which themselves took some 400 man-years to set up, and involved major changes to the part numbering, interchangeability data and demand levels. It also introduced new concepts like double entry and the ability to reverse parts.

Detailed requirements were first agreed in December 1985 and revolved around a decision to use bar codes (similar to those now firmly established in the retail trade) to identify all parts and stores locations. These bar codes, which are read by the system each time a part moves or a stock take is carried out, had to be applied to all drive tags, stores labels, bins and racks and included some half a million different part numbers, plus one-third of a million rack/bin location numbers and about 100,000 individual rotables. Parts were classified in three categories: R (repairable) parts made serviceable through overhaul or repair; E (expendable) items discarded and replenished by purchase or manufacture; and K (kits) parts made into kit form.

The formidable task of bar coding was started in January 1986 with stores racks and bins, and this was followed in May by the coding of every part in all stores and workshops locations. The 'big count' of all aeronautical parts was completed in July 1987.

In parallel with the introduction of TIME, British Airways has progressed a number of important enhancements to its materials management and forecasting techniques, comprising an on-going stock audit system, tighter control of free issues and a regular review of float levels. Another major development was implemented in workshop production control, featuring computer-produced bar-coded stage sheets, job-time recording, scheduling, priority assessment, capacity planning and on-line certification. At the peak of the highly concentrated activity in the creation of TIME, British Airways had 250 people, made up of engineering and computer staff, working full time on writing software and procedures, system testing, data clean-up, bar coding and a host of other related activities. Many others helped on a part-time basis, all contributing to one of the biggest short term tasks ever undertaken by the airline. TIME is changing the way British Airways Engineering goes about its business, making for higher efficiency and increased economic performance.

Aircraft Acceptance

The hand-over of a new aircraft may be accompanied by much ceremony and celebration, but before the champagne corks can be popped, much thorough work will have been put in by the manufacturer and customer alike to reach this early milestone in the life of a civil airliner.

After an aircraft has been assembled and the installation of systems, instruments, equipment and engines is complete, the manufacturer carries out standard function checks on the ground, which include sequencing of flying controls, engine runs, checking for fuel leaks, radio operation and many others. Any problems found will be rectified, maybe involving the changing of components. At this stage, the aircraft remains the property of the manufacturer. Most airline customers – and British Airways is no exception – have specialist quality engineers at the works to ensure that the airline's standards are met at each stage of the construction. These engineers are given access to these function tests, but their role is limited to being interested observers only, as these are the manufacturer's checks before the aircraft is made available to the customer for his acceptance.

After the ground checks have been completed, the aircraft commences a series of airborne tests, flown by a test pilot with support from test engineers and systems analysts. During the flight, all normal and emergency systems are checked, together with instrumentation and aircraft handling. If any significant deficiencies are found which require major adjustments or change of components, the aircraft will re-fly after rectification. One flight is rarely sufficient and there have been instances where more than 10 such flights were necessary before the aircraft was considered ready for presentation to the customer. Ready, that is, in the eyes of the manufacturer, for now the airline has official access to carry out its own checks. This process normally starts with a detailed ground inspection which may include everything from ensuring the overhead lockers close properly, flaps function as designed, to alignment of landing lights. This will take several hours, but may take a whole day. All defects, if any, are reported to the manufacturer, who is contractually bound to rectify these prior to the airline's flight test programme.

Although the aircraft remains under the control of the manufacturer's test pilot since it is still its property, the airline can exercise the option of using a flight test schedule to verify the soundness of aircraft and systems, based on its own experience. At the completion of the flight, any shortcomings must again be corrected by the manufacturer. In many cases, this will require another test flight in order to demonstrate that the problem has been solved. Typically, there will be two or three such flights before the airline is completely satisfied that the aircraft

Left:
Short-haul flights to Jersey are often flown by the BAC One-Eleven. *Tony Carre*

Bottom left:
Passengers'-eye view of Heathrow showing British Airways 747s in the terminal area below.

Right:
These motorists are in for a long wait as Boeing 747 *City of Elgin* crosses the road from British Airways' engineering complex at Hatton Cross. *Arthur Kemsley*

Below:
The long-range Lockheed TriStar 500 was employed on the routes to South America, serving Rio de Janeiro, São Paulo, Caracas and Bogotá. *British Airways/Adrian Meredith*

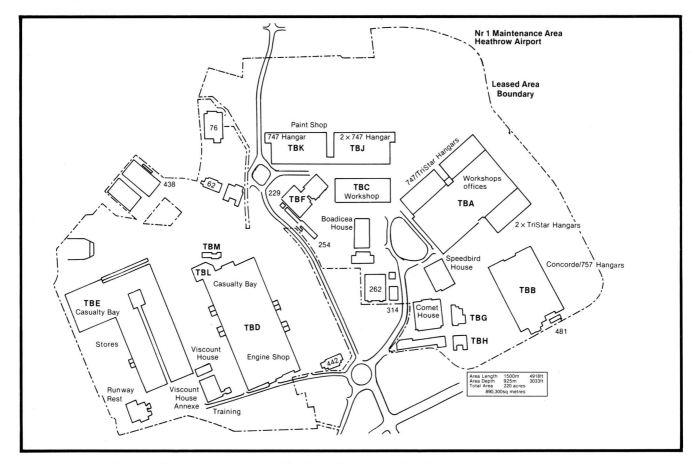

Nr 1 Maintenance Area
Heathrow Airport

Leased Area
Boundary

Paint Shop
747 Hangar **TBK**
2 x 747 Hangar **TBJ**

747/TriStar Hangars

Workshops
offices
TBA

TBC
Workshop

2 x TriStar Hangars

Boadicea
House

254

Concorde/757 Hangars

TBM

Speedbird
House

TBL

Casualty Bay

262

TBB

314

TBE
Casualty Bay

Comet
House
TBG

481

TBD

Stores

TBH

Viscount
House

Engine Shop

442

Runway
Rest

Viscount
House
Annexe

Training

Area Length	1500m	4918ft
Area Depth	925m	3033ft
Total Area	220 acres	
	890,300sq metres	

76

438   62

229

TBF

meets precisely its specification laid down at the time of the purchase order, or as modified during normal development.

The next step is the granting of a Certificate of Airworthiness (CofA) by the appropriate authority. In the case of a US manufacturer, this authority is vested in the Federal Aviation Agency (FAA). The UK equivalent is the Civil Aviation Authority (CAA). Money is then handed over by the customer airline and various legal, financial and technical documents will change hands to mark the title transfer. Only then can the aircraft be flown away by the customer. The same procedure is applied for each and every new aircraft purchased by British Airways before it is put onto its routes to carry fare-paying passengers.

Lifestation Lifeline

Within the engineering complex at Heathrow, a small team of engineering staff under the umbrella of the Line Spares Control Unit (LSCU), provides a lifeline between base and some 150 line stations as close as Brize Norton in Oxfordshire and as far away as Auckland, New Zealand. Their vital task is to fulfil the stations' often urgent needs for aircraft spares and equipment, which can range from a small nut and bolt to a giant RB211 engine.

Each station is issued with an Imprest, drawn up by Fleet Maintenance Production Planning, which lists what each should hold in order to keep the fleet in the air in all but the most unforeseen circumstances. The holding is different for virtually every station and is dependent on

London Heathrow engineering base

location, nature of operation, availability of local support, climate, aircraft types used, frequency of services and so on. A duplicate of each Imprest is held by the LSCU, and it is their responsibility to respond quickly to any demands against this listing and expedite shipping of the required part in the most efficient manner.

The very first thing to determine when receiving a request, known as a MOVEAD (Movement Advice), is the priority. All the stops are pulled out for an AOG (Aircraft on Ground), which is the most serious situation both in terms of cost and disruption to services. An IOR (Immediate Operational Requirement) is almost as urgent and the unit aims to dispatch the needed item within 24hrs. Other demands are dealt with in turn. On average, about 800 such demands are processed each month. Traffic is not only one way, however, as LSCU also has to ensure the rapid return of used parts to Heathrow.

The Special Projects Group, another part of LSCU, provides support to British Airways maintenance bases outside Heathrow, such as Gatwick, Manchester, Glasgow and Berlin, and keeps the Aircraft Recovery Unit going with all manner of spares, tools and equipment. The initial setting up of new line stations, or implementation of major changes to the requirements at existing stations, also come within its parameters. The alterations to the schedules twice a year, in April when the winter season changes to the summer and vice versa in October, is reflected in corresponding changes to the spares and equipment holding. Allocations are filled either from base or from another station if appropriate.

Another important function of the LSCU is to keep track of spares which are being loaned to other operators. During the course of a month, over 200 components are out on short-term loan, bringing in revenue in excess of £5 million a year. To a lesser extent, British Airways also borrows from other airlines but such items are removed from the aircraft as soon as practicable, usually on the next visit to base, and returned with the minimum of delay. In this way, the unit keeps the line stations going by maximising revenue and minimising expenditure.

Engineering Training

At Heathrow, British Airways provides all types of training for engineering staff to comply with rigid standards set by the CAA. A staff of around 100 includes 80 highly-qualified and experienced training officers whose connections with, or direct representation on relevant education, professional and training bodies, ensures the production of specialised programmes to meet all the airline's engineering training requirements. In a typical year the department copes with over 2,500 course members, 300 apprentices and more than 700 examination candidates, adding up to 30,000 adult man-days training at Heathrow, with another 3,000 abroad, plus 9,000 days for apprentice instruction. Major types of training offered include Basic Training, designed to provide an introduction to engineering concepts, procedures and new technology; Licence Without Type Rating, intended to augment and reinforce knowledge acquired through past experience; and Aircraft Type Authorisation, which prepares aircraft engineers for qualification on specific aircraft types.

The Apprentice Training School at Cranebank currently provides a three-year apprenticeship course covering aircraft engineering skills, technical education and practical experience. Achievement of the specified standards in all three elements constitute success in the scheme. Training programmes are available in avionics and mechanical trades, in either maintenance or overhaul. The training centre houses 18 discreet work areas providing the trainee with wide-ranging facilities to acquire skills in fitting, machine and assembly practices, undercarriages, structures, aircraft controls, avionic maintenance and wiring, hydraulic overhaul, heat processes, electronics, electrical and instrument overhaul, mechanical components and powerplant overhaul and maintenance. British Airways itself has a regular annual intake of 70 apprentices, with 30 course places available for the training of apprentices of other airlines or for government agencies. Revenue from this work approaches £2 million a year. Another £100,000 comes from Aircraft Type Authorisation training, which in the past has included training of RAF personnel on the TriStar and for a number of other customers.

British Airways also provides on-the-job training in aerospace application of non-destructive testing such as radiography, ultrasonics, eddy current, magnetic particle

and penetrant dye techniques, and can provide, for example, training in production planning where a standard course at a local college is combined with in-house training at the airline's various planning departments. Two-day up-date and refresher courses on live aircraft on line stations are a regular feature of off-base training. The development of skilled tradesmen has always received high priority within British Airways and forms an integral part of the CAA approval granted to the airline. This calls for suitably experienced craftsmen of sufficient numbers to undertake all likely volume and type of work appropriate to the approval. Once they join Engineering, tradesmen enter the Trade Advancement Scheme, comprising a series of courses leading to the Workshop Certificate or CAA Licence Without Type Rating. Each new person undergoes a five-day induction course which includes

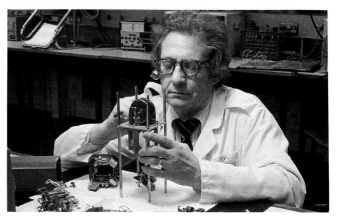

Above:
The Instrument Workshop includes a self-contained Clean Room for repair and overhaul of sensitive instrumentation.
British Airways

legislation, followed by familiarisation with procedures and documentation, which normally takes another 10 days.

All Engineering training is dominated by the conscious need for high standards, thoroughness and safety, and falls into two broad trade categories: Mechanical and Avionics. The mechanical trade is further subdivided to cover airframes, powerplants and associated electrics and instruments, while the avionics training specialises in imparting all the latest skills in electrics, instruments, radio and radar. None of these extensive engineering training programmes could function effectively without a number of important back-up units. These include administration offices, library, visual aids production, and the Training and Development Workshop. As well as building and maintaining training equipment, the workshop also gets involved in the development of prototype aircraft equipment.

Computer Based Training (CBT)

Beginning in 1984, British Airways embarked on a massive programme to convert some of its engineering courses for Computer Based Training (CBT), including Aircraft Engineering (AEC), Licence Without Type Rating (LWTR), Basic and Type Authorisation courses for the

To Fly, To Serve

Left:
British Airways takes special care of today's toddlers who may well become the business travellers of tomorrow.
British Airways/Adrian Meredith

Bottom left:
Checking-in at the new and impressive North Terminal at Gatwick. *British Airways*

Right:
British Airways flies the flag in its own terminal building at JFK International, New York, which is also home-from-home for a number of other airlines. *Author*

Bottom:
Reservations at Heathrow use the British Airways Booking System, or BABS for short, which handles 60,000 bookings a day. *British Airways/Adrian Meredith*

Bottom right:
Passengers disembark from a British Airways Boeing 747. *Arthur kemsley*

Boeing and Lockheed fleets. Specifications were developed and all instructional staff were trained in CBT authoring methods. The system was put into operation on 10 September 1986.

Although CBT has been in existence for at least 20 years, relatively convenient and cost-effective methods have only recently come on to the market. Even so, it takes British Airways some 30 man-days to produce the equivalent of a one-hour classroom lesson, working in teams of two with one instructor concentrating on authoring and lesson preparation, and another expert producing and editing the integrated video presentation. When one considers that this timespan is among the lowest ever achieved in this field, it is not difficult to see why it has only recently been introduced in Engineering Training.

The advantages are, of course, many. CBT is concise and structured to suit each student's individual requirements. The tutorial style lessons can be taken at or near the workplace, are available 16hrs a day, seven days a week, and allow the student to work at his or her own pace. It is also generally acknowledged that CBT is up to 50% more effective than live presentation.

The equipment in use by British Airways consists of four Author Stations incorporating a 16-colour VDU, colour video monitor, tape player and headphones for interactive use of video material; four similar colour student workstations; another 16 sets for Type training will be integrated with the Ground Maintenance Simulators (GMS), and 10 sets for Basic Training. Progressive implementation of these will be completed by 1989. Some 13% of the lesson material is or will be on video. The remainder is displayed on the VDU in colour, with directions to refer to notes or practice a skill on aircraft equipment or simulators as required. Each CBT lesson is combined with built-in test questions which provide an immediate progress check. Where Type Approval and Authorisation is at stake, a formal written examination is set as before. It is proposed to convert work-related training and special requirements into lessons for CBT, and the setting up of localised CBT stations for on-the-job training under the control of Line Managers, is also under consideration.

In spite of computerisation involving concentrated interaction with machines, students do not entirely lose personal contact with their human tutors. For AEC, LWTR and Basic courses, instructional staff who produced the lessons are available for reference by telephone or personal visit. For Type Authorisation courses, instructors are available at the students' workstations and also supervise and instruct the practical sessions on the GMS, which are an integral part of the course.

Ground Maintenance Simulators have been developed to demonstrate and practice a wide range of aircraft maintenance tasks from system operation which may include engine start/stop, engine running and refuelling procedures, to fault diagnosis and operation of built-in and portable maintenance test equipment. These highly sophisticated machines are able to simulate up to 280 faults across all systems. British Airways currently owns four simulators which are exact replicas in every detail of the cockpits of the airline's Boeing 737, 747, 757 and Lockheed L1011 TriStar jet aircraft. The TriStar GMS was the first of its kind in the world when introduced by British Airways in 1974.

Keeping Aircraft in the Air

Keeping aircraft safely in the air requires a vast amount of regular work on the ground, and while they may only be disappearing into the hangar once every few weeks, inspection of one form or another takes place after each landing. Most airline maintenance schedules are developed from recommended practices issued by the manufacturer after consultation with the appropriate airworthiness authority. These are updated from time to time through the issue of service bulletins by the manufacturer, or a change in the working practices by the airline operator. The following representative programme is based on the Lockheed TriStar, but proceeds along similar lines for other types in the British Airways fleet.

As soon as the TriStar touches down at an airport anywhere in the world, and each time it does so, it is subjected to a basic transit service which consists of a walkround visual inspection for any damage which may have been caused during the last sector flight. Such damage may be one of bird ingestion, icing in winter and tyre and brake wear. Engine oil levels are also checked and defects rectified. On the TriStar, this transit check will take some 30min after which the CAA and British Airways-approved qualified maintenance engineer puts his signature to the checklist to confirm that he has satisfied himself that the aircraft is serviceable and ready for its onward flight. Without this signature, the TriStar would have to remain grounded. The engineer also has limited authority, within the guidelines set out by the CAA, to carry minor defects over to a more convenient time and place. It must be emphasised, however, that this authorisation extends only to defects which in no way endanger the airworthiness of the aircraft.

Each subsequent stage in the maintenance cycle again incorporates a repeat of all previous checks, plus additional inspections, all dependent on flying hours and number of landings.

A Ramp 1 check is carried out as soon as the aircraft returns to its home base in London. This is almost identical in nature to those during transit stops and may additionally involve early lubrication of the undercarriage wheels.

Ramp 2 follows after 150 flying hours which, for the TriStar fleet, will occur from between 10-14 days. Around four to six engineering staff, drawn from both mechanical and avionics trades, will take some 3hrs to complete this more detailed service check, which also includes a look at starter motor oils, hydraulic fluids, flying control surfaces, flap extension and various aircraft systems. This is further added to in the Ramp 3 check which comes around after 300hrs, concentrating on making sure that any critical back-up systems such as standby electrical power and emergency lights, will actually work should the need arise. In view of the length of these checks, these are scheduled to be fitted in whenever the TriStar either remains in London overnight, or has a sufficiently long time on the ground between daytime flights.

Minor Maintenance

All checks up to and including Ramp 3 level are made during a stop-over on the ground, either at the Terminal or a parking area, but for the next step (classified as minor maintenance) the TriStar comes into the hangar. Known as Service 1 and Service 2, these occur every 850hrs and 1,600hrs respectively, and are taken care of in two and five eight-hour shifts, comprising 20-25 maintenance personnel per shift. In simple terms, this starts with changing oils, fluids and filters and lubricating just about everything that moves. A major feature is the internal inspection of the Rolls-Royce RB211 bypass turbofan engines by means of a boroscope, not unlike those used by the medical profession. The boroscope is inserted through tubes built into the inner core of the engine, to enable close-up examination of every turbine and compressor blade for cracks, erosion and broken parts. If anything is found outside acceptable tolerances, the RB211 is stripped down and rebuilt at the engine workshop at Heathrow. The engines are test-run prior to the aircraft receiving its final clearance.

This minor maintenance programme also provides the first opportunity to undertake a significant overall surveillance of the whole structure, looking particularly at the flap systems, doors, tail assembly and fuselage. It is also the first time that non-destructive testing methods are employed, for example, using X-rays to check for ingress of moisture in the elevators. Service 1 and 2 downtimes are additionally used to implement any changes and/or modifications originated by the manufacturer and based on in-service experience or problems encountered with other operators of the type. All checks incorporate various levels of internal cabin inspections to make sure that seats are not broken, toilets are in working order, overhead luggage racks close properly and numerous other inspections of this nature.

The Majors

The major maintenance schedule for the TriStar calls for Intercheck 1 and Intercheck 2 after 4,000 and 8,000 flying hours respectively. On the TriStar 1, flying primarily on high-density European routes, these milestones are reached after two and four years approximately. Both these checks keep the aircraft in the hangars for two weeks, using up around 7,000 man-hours each, and are usually fitted in during the winter period when aircraft utilisation is at its lowest in the year.

Major checks, and indeed Service 2, start with a good engineering wash, known as the 'deep clean', when the whole aircraft is given a thorough going over, particularly those areas which tend to get dirtier than others, such as

undercarriage bays, flying control surfaces, leading and trailing edges of the wing, engine intakes and the underbelly of the fuselage. The main reason for this is to assist the initial inspections which are a fundamental part of any major maintenance. It is these inspections which generate the bulk of the rectification work.

A detailed examination of the aircraft structure based on an agreed structural inspection programme laid down by the CAA and the manufacturer, internal corrosion of the belly hold and tests galore of all protection standby systems, form the principal elements of major maintenance. An Intercheck is also the time for changing components. These, like undercarriages, have a fixed lifespan but the majority of others, among them interior furnishings such as seats and carpets, are replaced 'on condition'. For the structural check, the TriStar is substantially taken apart, with work concentrating on the insides of the wings, tail fins and fuselage crown. These are all areas where it is not normally expected to find damage and the necessary tasks are spread on a proportional basis between Interchecks 1 and 2. The belly of an aircraft is notoriously prone to corrosion as a result of condensation and fluid spillage, particularly in the vicinity of the galleys, toilets and from vulnerable freight, and is regularly inspected. A protective spray coating minimises this potential hazard. Another part of the Majors requirement is a more comprehensive check by the NDT (non-destructive testing) section, supplementing the visual inspection of the main structure and components, notably flying control surfaces.

'Milestone Charts' – simple critical path programme sheets – are in widespread use on all Service and Interchecks to control working methods in order to make more efficient use of manpower and keep within the planned downtime of the aircraft. These charts enable the daily progress of each check to be recorded and monitored against the projected plan. On average, the TriStar 1 is out of service on maintenance no more than 11 total days a year, and for the TriStar 200, it is 22 days.

Service intervals, man-hour requirements and specific maintenance tasks will vary from type to type, but every aircraft across the British Airways fleet will receive the same comprehensive and thorough attention, so that when it leaves the hangar with its Certificate of Maintenance Release, it is as good as new.

The TriStar Fleet

Model and Number in Service	Hours Flown to Date*	Landings Made to Date	Average Landings Per Month
L1011-1(9)	198,718	9,994	574
L1011-200(8)	161,649	41,432	412
L1011-500(2)‡	27,355	6,707	144
Total (19)	387,722	58,133	1,130

*31 December 1986
‡The 500s have since left the fleet.

Productivity improvements are currently being implemented in the aircraft hangars in the form of MPCS, which

They Also Serve — 2

Right:
In the final moments before departure the Ramp Co-ordinator supervises operations. *British Airways/Adrian Meredith*

Below:
Engine overhaul is a vital part of engineering and is undertaken both at Heathrow and by British Airways Engine Overhaul Ltd in South Wales.
British Airways/Adrian Meredith

Engineering Excellence — 2

Right:
Vertical assembly of the Concorde Olympus engine at the Engine Shop at Heathrow.
British Airways/Adrian Meredith

Below:
One of British Airways' fleet of BAC One-Elevens is repainted in the new airline livery.
British Airways/Adrian Meredith

stands for Maintenance and Control System, and OMEGA – Overhaul and Maintenance Engineering for Aircraft. While MPCS is a manual system as against the computerised OMEGA, both are complementary with the same objectives – the optimisation of efficiency in the utilisation of resources. MPCS is a structured means of allocating resources needed to accomplish specific work packages. The main elements are planning, production control and management reporting, and it is the long-term plan which gives rise to the input standards for specific aircraft from which the milestone programme is constructed. OMEGA embraces the provision of worksheets, job cards and clearance sheets. It will also be used to plan the availability of labour, materials, tools, equipment and technical information such as drawings, service bulletins and service newsletters. The heart of the system is the Job Data Base which contains the Production Engineering response to every scheduled task likely to arise on the aircraft. Also already on stream is work packaging, where OMEGA selects all the jobs requiring action at each maintenance check, and prior to this, produces a list of tools and equipment requirements to check availability in advance of need. Further development phases will introduce job time recording, production control, post-aircraft check analysis and feasibility planning programmes.

Looking Good

The appearance of an aircraft, and in the first instance the external livery, provides the passenger with a lasting impression of the airline he or she is flying with, but there is much more to painting than meets the eye. All aircraft in the British Airways fleet are given the same basic treatment which normally lasts approximately four to five years, with a small element of touching-up in between times. Apart from making the aircraft look smart, painting is also the best way of minimising corrosion of the outer surfaces. The process adopted by British Airways has been arrived at by a combination of trials and experience.

The aircraft is firstly pre-washed by the Chemical Cleaning Unit before the paint stripper is sprayed on, making sure that all non-metallic surfaces like windows, orifices, engine intakes, landing gear etc, are masked to protect them from the effects of the stripper. Scraping and hosing down with high-pressure water jets then removes all the top coat and most of the primer – the rest has to be rubbed down by hand. When considering that on a 747 Jumbo the painted surface area is equivalent to more than 100 family cars, the size of the task facing the workmen becomes fairly apparent. 'Edge' stripping then carefully removes the paint to the very edge of vulnerable surfaces, and after a thorough rinse the non-metallic areas of the exterior (extensive on a modern aircraft) are rubbed down by hand and any damage from stripping is made good. A further shampoo and rinse precedes the conversion coating which consists of a careful application of an acid anodising fluid. The aircraft is now ready for painting.

The all-important epoxy resin primer comes first, giving not only protection but providing also a key for the two

finishing coats of paint, starting with the pearl grey upper fuselage, followed by the midnight blue on the fin, lower fuselage and engine casings. Next comes the red Speedwing and fin flash. The coat of arms and a multitude of other external markings such as aircraft registration, are applied in decal form or by stencil. Plane painting relies on cleanliness and controlled temperatures, but above all on good teamwork for acceptable results, as consistency over large areas is not easy to achieve. Great emphasis is placed on health and safety precautions, as potential hazards when using stripper and spray paint are many. Standards and facilities in the paintshops are constantly being improved, helping to increase third party work which also extends to a washing and polishing service for aircraft up to TriStar size.

The external paint scheme is but one aspect of the airline's objective of possessing the smartest looking airliners in the world. Exterior and interior condition and general cleanliness throughout are of equal importance to the appearance of the aircraft and ultimate presentation to the passenger. Priorities have been set to focus on the areas immediately round the passenger seats (clean ashtrays, tables, carpets, window surrounds), toilets, galleys, flightdeck and on a thorough overall nightstop clean to ensure that each aircraft goes out looking good and smelling fresh in the morning.

British Airways Engine Overhaul Limited

The origins of British Airways Engine Overhaul Ltd can be traced back as far as 1924 to the establishment of the Imperial Airways engine workshops at Croydon. In more than 60 years since, the company has built up a growing

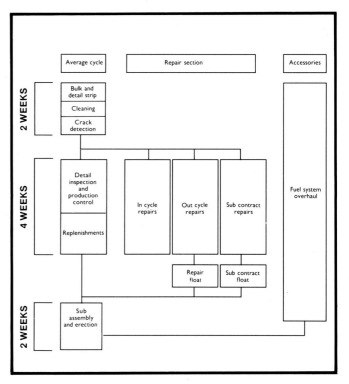

Typical engine overhaul cycle

90

reputation for skill and expertise to earn itself a place among the best engine overhaul operations in the world.

It presently has two plants in South Wales some nine miles outside Cardiff, at Treforest in the beautiful Taff Valley and at nearby Nantgarw on the Caerphilly road. A new high-technology plant is under construction at the existing site at Nantgarw. It is due for completion by spring 1989 and will replace the Treforest factory which is now almost 50 years old. All engine overhaul facilities will then be grouped together in one place, providing a total working area of 328,000sq ft (30,400sq m). The choice of South Wales was dictated by the exigencies of the war years, when every activity of vital importance to the war effort was evacuated to remoter locations for safety reasons. The excellent motorway links via the M4 to Heathrow Airport present no problems of distance today.

BEOL has the capabilities for a comprehensive overhaul and repair service of more than 20 aero engines ranging from small auxiliary power units (APUs) to mighty bypass engines developing a massive 53,000lb (231kN) thrust. The major powerplants include the Olympus 593/610 turbojet which drives Concorde to twice the speed of sound; four variants of the Rolls-Royce RB211 turbofans fitted to British Airways Boeing 747s and 757s and Lockheed TriStars; the Pratt and Whitney JT9D turbofan installed in the Boeing 747 and the most popular of all, the JT8D, in service worldwide on almost 5,000 aircraft including the Boeing 737 and 727 and McDonnell Douglas DC-9 and MD-80 series. Two of the older types still regularly overhauled are the Pratt and Whitney JT3D which powers the Boeing 707 and Douglas DC-8 airliners and the Rolls-Royce Conway, now only in service with the RAF on the VC10 and Victor tankers. Work on the JT3D will be discontinued once current contracts have been fulfilled. The smaller Rolls-Royce Spey engine used on the One-Eleven and work on the Dart turboprop are contracted out. The APU currently handled is the Garrett AiResearch GTCP 660. In addition to the engines themselves, BEOL's expertise also encompasses ancillaries such as fuel pumps, fuel control systems (FCUs) and many other accessories. Fuel control systems and fuel pumps are highly complex pieces of machinery. An FCU governs engine starting, acceleration and deceleration, and maintains the selected engine speeds in all conditions of flight. Fuel pumps are subjected in service to a punishing routine of delivering large quantities of fuel, up to 26,000lb an hour on a JT9D, and at very high pressures up to 1,100psi. The fuel systems workshop has 38 staff including supervisors, and between them they are responsible for a large range of components with thousands of part numbers. The shop produces over 350 FCUs and 300 fuel pumps a year and also handles more than 3,000 other components of all shapes and sizes. Work can vary from the incredibly complex JT9D FCU to a simple valve or filter. Extensive testing sometimes involves running the components at varying speeds, durations, pressures, flows and temperatures for many hours at a time, and the results must meet a very high degree of accuracy.

Incoming engines are stripped, cleaned and minutely checked for wear and tear, using a mixture of highly sophisticated techniques such as X-ray and ultraviolet crack detection, together with expert visual inspection. The integrity of each major component is verified using the most up-to-date non-destructive testing methods which include eddy current, ultrasonic, magnaflux and electrostatic testing. Engine parts found to be faulty (90% of failures have been shown to be material orientated), or no longer within the tolerances specified by the manufacturer, can often be reclaimed using the latest techniques. Among these are plasma spraying, orbital machine welding, vacuum brazing, electron beam welding, electroplating and inert gas welding. The development of this specialisation has resulted in vast savings in replacement costs for customers and has propelled the company to the top in this particular field. When considering that the average overhaul cost for a single JT9D engine amounts to more than £600,000 of which 80% is cost of materials, the benefits are not difficult to see. Each JT9D consists of 60,000 parts. The major costs are reflected in the turbine area, but if the large cases and many other parts were not repairable, the costs would be astronomic. BEOL also generally adopts much more stringent criteria – closer tolerances equate to higher efficiency – and this results in further service economies.

Parts that have been repaired, or replacement parts, undergo another thorough check before being returned to the assembly lines. Following completion and static inspection, each engine is tested in one of three test bed facilities which cover all engine types currently in service. One has been uprated for testing to 100,000lb (445kN) thrust.

A sophisticated computer stock control system is in operation which allows not only careful monitoring of its extensive stocks of spare engine components, but also speedy requisition of parts through direct computer access. With manufacturers in the UK and the USA, such control is very necessary in order to meet contracted turn-round times. The same computer system 'Rework', also monitors and controls all parts undergoing repair. Some components undergo over 60 operations in their repair cycle, and each is individually signed off by qualified staff. The system will show all of the parts of any particular type that is under repair, and exactly how far from completion each one is at that moment. A complete engine overhaul cycle from strip down to test is typically 8-10 weeks, ranking among the best in the business.

BEOL has a total workforce of 900, most of whom are highly-skilled operatives and managers who have been with the company a long time. To ensure continuity of staff with the right expertise for the present and the future, an apprenticeship scheme is in operation, which provides places for 10 school leavers each year. Training facilities are also available for the staff of outside customers, as is the complete range of engine overhaul services. Third party work now brings in approximately £30 million revenue a year.

Left:

Fly by wire: one of the first A320 Airbuses to be delivered to British Airways following the B Cal takeover. *Adrian Meredith*

Far left:

The name of B.Cal lives on in the new charter company Caledonian Airways which has absorbed British Airtours and the smaller charter element of British Caledonian. Seen here is Lockheed TriStar 385 G-BBAJ newly outshopped in the Caledonian Airways livery. *G. P. & C. M. Dobson*

Below:

Full power ahead: it is confidently expected that B Cal will earn British Airways a minimum of £400 million in extra revenue.

Here we see former BCal DC-10-30 G-BEBL newly repainted in British Airways' livery. *Colin Wood*

9 Caledonian Airways – The Smartest way to the Sun

Caledonian Airways came into being in August 1969 as BEA Airtours, later British Airtours and by 1987 had expanded to become the third largest charter operator in the UK, employing 1,650 people and carrying more than 2.5 million passengers a year. The present name became effective on 1 April 1988 when the charter only activities of British Airtours were combined with the smaller charter element of British Caledonian. Although a wholly-owned subsidiary of British Airways, it operates as a separate entity, with its headquarters at London's Gatwick Airport and a second base at Manchester. Financially, it also stands alone and has been consistently profitable. Service and operational standards are among the highest in the business, and a long way from the somewhat tarnished image of charter airlines that existed not so many years ago.

Airtours' foundation as a subsidiary of the national flag-carrier undoubtedly gave it a head start, but there were other fortuitous factors that contributed to a successful launch. With the build-up of the Trident fleet bringing to an end scheduled Comet operations in March 1969, British European Airways (BEA) was presented with a golden opportunity to gain a quick foothold in the lucrative European inclusive-tours charter market without the need for the massive expenditure usually associated with the purchase of aircraft when setting up a new airline. Ten Comet 4Bs were thus delivered to Gatwick in January 1970 to form the initial fleet of the newly-formed BEA Airtours and the first charter was flown between Gatwick and Palma de Mallorca on 6 March that same year, in good time for the coming summer season. The decision to enter the fiercely competitive charter world proved justified and in the first year the Comets carried some 600,000 passengers, with more than half of the flights destined for Spain, the favourite place in the sun for the British holiday-maker.

The new airline was soon looking towards the North American charter market, making plans to put its two Boeing 707-436s (acquired from BOAC in the spring of 1972) onto the Atlantic beginning with the 1973 season. Protracted licence negotiations with the American authorities, however, delayed this introduction by one year, leaving British Airtours – as it was then known – with surplus capacity, especially following the purchase of a further five 707s from BOAC in early 1973. This difficult situation did much to hasten the end of the Comets which were retired after completing a last flight from Paris to Gatwick on 31 October 1973.

In the meantime, British Airtours had entered into a contract with Syrian Arab Airlines to operate some of that airline's scheduled passenger services. For two years, two 707s in Syrian Arab markings flew on several routes out of Damascus, including that to London via Athens, Rome and Frankfurt; to Tripoli, Cairo, Jeddah and Sana'a; and to Karachi and Delhi with stops at Abu Dhabi and Dubai. Another agreement with DETA of Mozambique saw British Airtours flying for eight months between Lourenco Marques (now Maputo), Beira and Lisbon.

The 'Hadj', when Muslims from all over the world embark on a religious pilgrimage to the holy shrine at Mecca in Saudi Arabia, was another area where the airline made its presence felt. At one time it had five 707s stationed at Teheran, operating nonstop throughout the day between the Iranian capital and Jeddah. These flights were very profitable but had to end as the Hadj moved into the summer, when aircraft were fully committed to European inclusive-tours and transatlantic charter programmes.

Towards the end of the decade, British Airtours' fleet of nine 707s were flying extensive European charters for a wide variety of major tour operators, from both Manchester and Gatwick Airports, coupled with long-haul flights to the US West Coast, Canada and the Far East, with the occasional excursions also to the Caribbean and South America. Scheduled services were conducted on behalf of Air Mauritius between Plaisance and Bombay via Seychelles, and to London with stops at Nairobi and Rome. Charter passengers carried approached the one million mark in a one-year period. On the non-flying front, a substantial airline handling business was being developed at Gatwick, not only for its own operations, but also for other airlines.

As fuel costs continued to spiral, economics began to price the 707s out of the market, forcing British Airtours to look for new aircraft. In parallel with British Airways, an order was placed for nine advanced Boeing 737-236 twin-jets, the first of which was handed over to the airline in March 1980. The replacement programme was completed the following year with the delivery of the ninth 737, together with two large-capacity Lockheed L1011-200 TriStars. TriStar Series 1s were later substituted for the Series 200. A promising, if short-lived, LondonGatwick-Newark service was inaugurated on 1 April 1981 and flown three times a week with 707s until axed in a policy reversal the following August. It did not take long before this route was snapped up by People Express, later also joined by Virgin Atlantic Airways. The cessation of the Newark flights also heralded the withdrawal of the older Boeing jets.

In recent years, the Gatwick business had additionally included scheduled services operated on behalf of British Airways to 21 destinations in Europe, North Africa and the Caribbean. Many of these were scheduled 'leisure' routes, flown predominantly to Spain and Italy.

An event of significance was the inaugural use of a four-engined Boeing 747-200B Jumbo jet to service the growing charter programme to the USA and Canada. This helped to strengthen the airline's position in the UK intercontinen-tal charter league and provided an excellent launch for British Airways' newest tour company, Poundstretcher which, as a result, managed to record a successful first year. Total revenue earned by British Airtours at that time was nudging the £100 million mark.

Today, the fleet comprises four TriStars and four 737s, operating charter flights to destinations principally in the Mediterranean area. Two 231-seat Rolls-Royce-powered Boeing 757-200s will join the fleet in Spring 1989.

High Profile

In its relatively short history, the airline has developed a varied spread of activities but it is as a holiday airline that it is known best. There is hardly a single European holiday airport where its aircraft have not made an appearance at one time or other during the seasons, and this is reflected in over two million passengers and 20,000 flights per year, which calls for a high level of planning activity. The process usually begins as early as May for the following year's programme, when the tour companies approach the airline to provide the air transport element for their package holidays. Starting with empty aircraft and a clean sheet covering the period from 1 April to 31 October for the summer schedule, dates are gradually filled in and by July/August, every day will, hopefully, be booked solid. This is no easy task since on short-haul operations, which take up most of Caledonian's capacity, each aircraft is allocated three flight 'slots', dividing up into morning, afternoon and night sectors.

The European inclusive-tours business stands or falls by a successful implementation of what is referred to, tongue-in-cheek, as the 'hot beds' policy, which means that tourists need to arrive at the same time as hotels are vacated by previous groups. This results in specific changeover days, usually at the weekend and beginning of the week, when whole armadas of aircraft swoop down

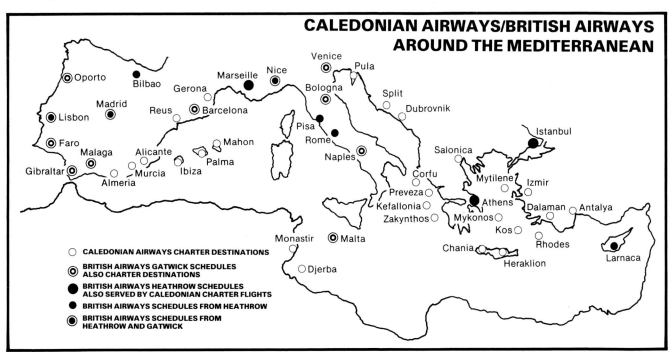

CALEDONIAN AIRWAYS/BRITISH AIRWAYS AROUND THE MEDITERRANEAN

○ CALEDONIAN AIRWAYS CHARTER DESTINATIONS

◎ BRITISH AIRWAYS GATWICK SCHEDULES ALSO CHARTER DESTINATIONS

● BRITISH AIRWAYS HEATHROW SCHEDULES ALSO SERVED BY CALEDONIAN CHARTER FLIGHTS

● BRITISH AIRWAYS SCHEDULES FROM HEATHROW

◉ BRITISH AIRWAYS SCHEDULES FROM HEATHROW AND GATWICK

Architects
of Success

**Lord King of Wartnaby, who took over as British
Airways Chairman from Sir Ross Stainton on
1 February 1981, has presided over the major
turnaround in the airline's financial performance
over the last six years through a programme of drastic
rationalisation coupled with an increased emphasis
on marketing and customer.**
British Airways/Adrian Meredith

**In February 1983, Colin Marshall (now Sir Colin)
teamed up with Lord King when he was appointed as
Chief Executive in succession to Roy Watts.**
British Airways/Adrian Meredith

Above:
BEA Airtours had a successful and profitable first year of operation with its fleet of nine de Havilland Comet 4Bs.
British Airways/Adrian Meredith

in near formation, leaving the airfield almost deserted on other days. Corfu, which cannot take the TriStar, has 35 flights a week, 30 of which arrive on Monday!

The midweek troughs have to be filled with whatever other charter work can be found. Fortunately there are an increasing number of companies, societies and well-heeled individuals who go in for whole-plane charters, using the aircraft for promotional purposes, as incentives and rewards for sales staff and for educational, sporting and even ego trips. A special charter department deals with hiring out any of the British Airways and Caledonian aircraft. Concorde, a particular favourite, would cost around £100,000 for a day.

High standards of in-flight catering are demanded by Caledonian Airways from its contracted suppliers. In selecting the menus to be offered, careful consideration is given to regional preferences; food served out of Manchester may differ to that on flights from Gatwick. When the holiday is over, passengers are known to prefer traditional English fare on the way home. Special school trips are notable for an abundance of sausages, beefburgers and chips. What is perhaps not always appreciated by the passenger is the fact that it is the tour operator who makes the actual choice from the available menu, depending on the budgeted allowance for food within his total holiday cost. Unhappily, when a passenger is dissatisfied with only receiving a cup of tea and biscuits on a four-hour flight to the Canary Islands, anger is often directed misguidedly at the airline. The answer is not to change the airline, but to book the next holiday with a different tour company.

Within the total profit earned by Caledonian Airways, some 20% is derived from duty-free sales on board the aircraft. This is a surprisingly significant element of income, and the airline carries a commensurately large selection of duty-free goods.

The Caledonian Domain

British Airways' own and other major tour operators Intasun, and Thomson, are responsible for more than half of the airline's business. The remainder comes from other tour companies, both large and small.

The regional distribution of traffic is slowly changing in emphasis as a result of the opening up of new areas, such as the Aegean, increasing the choice of holidays. Spain, nevertheless – the traditional market especially for the British holiday-maker – still leads the field with 39%. Greece is moving up the table having captured a 19% share. The rest is made up in smallish chunks from flights to Turkey, Italy, Portugal, Yugoslavia, Tunisia and Morocco.

A dozen Spanish towns and cities regularly play host to Caledonian Airways aircraft. Bilbao and Madrid are mostly business orientated, while Barcelona and Malaga, all British Airways scheduled destinations, also support a large amount of charter traffic. Other popular Spanish holiday airports served are Gerona, Reus, Murcia, Alicante, Santiago and Almeria, together with the island points of Mahon, Palma and Ibiza in the Balearics. Further along the Iberian Peninsula, Caledonian serves Gibraltar and Faro, Lisbon and Oporto in Portugal, as well as reaching across to the North African coast where frequent ports of call are Djerba and Monastir in southern Tunisia. Off the west coast of Africa can be found Funchal in the Portuguese Madeira Islands and Arrecife, Las Palmas and Tenerife in the Canaries. All are served frequently with TriStars and 737s. Austrian, Swiss, French and Italian routes are served, while further east, Pula, Split and Dubrovnik give access to the Adriatic resorts along the Yugoslav coast.

As mentioned already, two of the growth areas are the Greek and Turkish resorts, particularly in the Aegean. Where less than 10 years ago services were only possible to Corfu, Heraklion, Rhodes and Athens, there are now suitable airfields at Preveza/Lefkas, Kefallonia, Zakynthos, Skiathos, Chania, Mytilene, Samos, Mykonos, Araxos, Kos, Salonica, and a few others not presently on Caledonian's schedule. In Turkey, the preferred places are Izmir, Dalaman and Antalya along the coast.

During wintertime, the European operation switches from the sandy beaches of the Med to the ski slopes of the Alps and Pyrenees. Traffic to the Greek islands – and to a lesser extent to Spain – drops off considerably, though the Canary Islands, which can boast pleasantly warm winter sun, remain buoyant. Among the busiest routes are those from Gatwick and Manchester to Salzburg in Austria, which is tremendously popular with school parties off on their annual skiing holidays.

Excellent Aircraft in Good Hands

The present Caledonian fleet consists of four Lockheed L1011 TriStars and four Boeing 737-200, based at Manchester for the summer season, and at the Caledonian hangar complex at the edge of Gatwick Airport.

The popular 737s differ from the mainstream British Airways aircraft in having a higher take-off weight and an all-tourist layout for 128 passengers.

The wide-bodied TriStar is fitted out with a flight management system which not only greatly enhances its operational safety, but also guides the aircraft along the most fuel-efficient flight path. Onboard flight data recording programmes continually monitor and analyse all aspects of flight performance on every flight. An automatic blind landing system to Category III enables safe operation in even the most atrocious weather conditions. The 737 is similarly equipped and both types are also fitted with high frequency radio to provide direct communication with base from anywhere on the network.

Fully loaded with 393 passengers, the Caledonian TriStars have a range of 4,200 miles (6,800km) and can cruise at 610mph (985km/h). The short-haul 737 on the other hand has a typical range of 1,800 miles (2,900km). The two types share the Mediterranean charters, although the big TriStar is not able to land at some of the smaller fields such as Antalya, Corfu, Funchal, Reus and Verona, where the dumpy little Boeing jet reigns supreme.

Caledonian Airways is planning to upgrade and develop its fleet by adding the narrow-bodied Boeing 757 to bridge the large capacity gap between the 737 and the TriStar. Two Rolls-Royce-powered 757-200s, configured for 231 passengers in an all-economy layout, are on order for delivery in the Spring of 1989, with more to follow as the traffic develops.

All the stops are pulled out in looking after the fleet. At the Gatwick base, British Airways employs highly-skilled staff at its engineering complex which includes avionics and mechanical workshops to deal with the Caledonian fleet. Non-destructive testing services are provided by an outside contractor. Full maintenance is carried out on its Boeing 737 twins and up to Interchecks on the TriStars. For their 'Majors', the latter goes into the British Airways hangars at Heathrow. Should an engine have to be replaced on any aircraft, this is carried out by Engineering at Gatwick. Engine overhaul is undertaken by another British Airways subsidiary, BEOL (British Airways Engine Overhaul Ltd), situated at Nantgarw in South Wales. Caledonian can, of course, call upon the full technological back-up from the parent company at all times.

Maintenance schedules are broadly in line with those of British Airways mainline aircraft, but the Caledonian operating pattern dictates certain variations, strictly within the guidelines laid down by the manufacturers and the CAA. The high-frequency, largely short-haul, charter business where a day's service allocation for each aircraft may involve as many as three round trips, demands that the aircraft spend as little time as possible on the ground. This is achieved by 'equalising' maintenance (especially on higher-time 'Service' and 'Interchecks') into single eight-hour shifts, usually worked when flying activities are in any case drastically curtailed. What this means is that on a Service 3 check, fixed at 3,200hrs on the TriStars for example, the eight-hour work package may be made up of half the 1,600hrs Service 2 check, one-quarter of Service 3 and one-quarter of the next major 4,000hrs Intercheck 1,

Above:
'Caledonian Girls' ready for take-off in their Lockheed L1011 TriStar.
Caledonian Airways via Scot Gold Blyth

completing each full service in instalments, as it were. A complete Intercheck 1 would have a normal downtime of 12 days. The schedule is, of course, carefully worked out to comply in all respects with regulations laid down for each stage. In spite of all today's high-technology sophistication, people are still needed to fly the aircraft and to ensure the well-being of the passengers aboard. Minimum length of flying experience among the Caledonian pilots is 14 years, and a captain has to have at least 20 years before gaining that extra stripe. Many can look back to anything up to 30 years in the cockpit, but no matter how long or how experienced an individual may be, everyone has to do a twice-yearly update course on the aircraft simulator, in addition to an annual in-flight check. A simulator is a highly-complex, computerised mock-up of the flightdeck that can faithfully reproduce any contingencies likely to happen in flight, or during take-off and landing.

Thorough training is also the hallmark of the cabin crew, both male and female, whose job may have an air of glamour, but also involves a lot of dedicated hard work. Every flight is under the control of a Cabin Service Officer who looks after the cabin attendants (10 or 11 in a TriStar), duty-free sales and the well-being of the passengers.

Most of Caledonian services are of relatively short duration, making it possible for the crew to fly out and back on the same day. Exceeding the maximum permissible shift of 12½hrs will mean an overnight stay, but even the crew will admit that at the majority of the airline's regular destinations, this is no great hardship.

Nothing left to Chance

Whenever a new holiday destination is proposed for inclusion in the summer or winter programmes, both tour companies and potential air carriers sit down together to examine the feasibility of such an operation. There can be many factors giving rise to difficulties but discussions invariably come back to the airfield. It may be thought that, provided the runway is long and strong enough for the Caledonian fleet, everything is ready to go – far from it. A thorough investigation may have to be initiated, during which Caledonian Airways will assess and evaluate all aspects of the operation in order to satisfy itself of the safety and advisability of its use.

The airline works by three airport classifications: A) Unrestricted; B) Requiring a Brief; and C) Requiring a Visit.

Class 'A' is self-explanatory and applies principally to established airports which lack none of the necessary

Below:
Routine maintenance on a Pratt & Whitney JT8D engine oil system; the JT8D powers the 737.
British Airtours

facilities and services, and are capable of accepting any aircraft pencilled in for the route.

Class 'B' may be an airfield that has some unusual features, details of which need to be brought to the attention of the air crew. These will be covered in an Airfield Briefing Sheet, prepared by Flight Management assisted by the British Airways Route Briefing Unit, which may highlight such things as possible turbulence and windshear resulting from the formation of the terrain along the approach; the types of radar installations, landing aids and communications; restrictions pertaining to the over-flying of the adjacent town, night flying regulations and the likelihood of early morning fog. It may not have fuel, in which case enough has to be carried on the aircraft for the entire return journey or for a stop-over nearby. As this can reduce the passenger payload, it may make the whole operation uneconomical for the tour operator.

A Class 'C' airfield is one where after all such difficulties have been assessed, the airline still feels that caution is in order and wishes to make further on-the-spot investigations before committing itself to the client. The first Caledonian Airways crew to visit such a field will always consist entirely of management staff who will prepare, wherever possible, an audio-visual brief immediately upon return. Line pilots will join management on a follow-up flight, taking over fully only thereafter. Nothing therefore is left to chance.

Once an aircraft has landed, engineering maintenance aspects take over the safe operation. Number one priority is to establish the availability, or otherwise, of local support with the necessary expertise to undertake transit checks, refuelling and emergency repair work, and the capacity to handle the proposed frequency of operation. Usually, where another major operator is based at the field, Caledonian Airways will evaluate facilities, equipment, staff and standards and having satisfied itself that its basic stipulations can be met, will then enter into a technical handling agreement with that company. The agreement may be for full technical handling services, or support handling such as that provided in the Greek islands by Olympic Airways, a long-time associate of Airtours and BEA before, which provides for limited technical and spares assistance. By choice, any emergency spares back-up will be handled by Gatwick, but where more practicable these may be supplied by a neighbouring station or obtained on loan from another airline based in the vicinity with the same type of aircraft fleet. Full Technical Handling demands the presence of a Licensed Engineer in compliance with CAA legislative requirements, who is fully qualified to carry out any work on the Caledonian fleet from routine servicing to casualty repairs.

The Engineering Quality Manager has full authority to approve a local handling organisation or individual

Left:
Pre-flight checks on a Boeing 747 undercarriage bay. This aircraft was used for a time by British Airtours but now flies in British Airways colours.
British Airways

Caledonian's TriStar fleet consists of four aircraft fitted out for 393 passengers.
Caledonian Airways via Scott Gold Blyth

engineer. This approval may be forthcoming by accepting another country's or airline's aviation authority standards after a full technical evaluation, or by training a local technician employed by the airline carrying out the technical handling.

Where an airfield is totally devoid of support facilities, or where no immediate assistance can be obtained from nearby stations, Caledonian Airways will carefully assess the operational risks associated with flying into such an airfield. In order to overcome potential problems without in any way compromising the safety of passengers and crew, the airline has several options. It may, for example, decide to position a flying engineer on the aircraft who will undertake the transit turnround inspection and refuelling operation. A flight spares pack will also be carried on board, containing a limited selection of items most likely to be needed such as wheels, jacks, technical spares, fluid systems replenishment tools and hydraulic repair kits.

On short-distance flights the task of carrying out transit checks and supervising refuelling may be given to the crew, who will have been suitably familiarised with these procedures. In this situation, the aircraft will receive detailed additional maintenance checks before it leaves the UK and again the moment it returns, making particularly sure that tyres are not worn down and oxygen, hydraulic and oil systems are more fully topped up than is normally required. Izmir-Gigli, one of the newest airfields to be opened to IT traffic, is one such location. Crew turnround is, however, limited to the Boeing 737.

At some of the busier locations like Malaga, which will be served around 850 times during the holidays with both 737s and TriStars, the airline employs its own maintenance personnel, typically three or four operatives drawn from the avionics and mechanical trades; at Stockholm for example a British Airways scheduled destination, the airline has an arrangement with Lufthansa for the provision of full technical support. Apart from routine matters, Lufthansa's licensed engineer will also check the technical log for any minor defects which may have been carried over, and which are within his authority to put right, should this be considered prudent prior to the aircraft's return to its home base.

Flight crew carrying out start-up drills on the Boeing 737 prior to departure.

10 British Airways – To be the Best

The process of creating the British Airways of today was begun in 1981 with the appointment of Lord King of Wartnaby as Chairman, charged with the difficult task of steering the airline towards profitability, to be followed by privatisation at the earliest possible opportunity, in line with government policy. At the time the new man took over, British Airways was losing money and its reputation among the travelling public was not enjoying the most favourable comparisons, in terms of efficiency and customer service, with some of the major competitors. This also coincided with a general slump throughout the international airline industry, highlighted by a decline in passenger volumes forcing down fares and reducing the real value of income. In order to get back to profitability with the utmost speed, it became necessary to substantially reduce capital expenditure and operating costs, and to improve efficiency. Rationalisation of the aircraft fleet and drastic pruning of staff from some 51,000 to under 36,000 within two years, almost entirely by means of an incentive-based voluntary scheme, were the obvious outward and highly-publicised signs. British Airways also divested itself of some of its shareholdings in other companies, including subsidiaries. As a direct result of this savage cost-cutting programme, British Airways was back in profit by 1983.

A central pivot of the airline's approach was a determination to improve its service to the customer. The initial 'Putting People First' campaign involved the training of 14,000 staff across the airline, whose jobs bring them into direct contact with the customer. Its purpose was to focus attention on the needs of the passenger in particular, on identifying the role of staff within the airline, and in finding ways of improving service all round. The complete redesign of the corporate image soon after was a further significant step down this long and winding road. Reaction from the passenger today and from the industry, which has heaped honour after honour on the airline in recent times, confirms that this particular strategy has been a great success.

The airline was not, however, out of the wood yet. The eagerly awaited CAA review of UK aviation policy, published in July 1984, called for a reduction of British Airways' monopoly, and the opening up of more routes to competition between the UK airlines. Just what the government ordered, one would have thought. Not a bit of it. After much – and often acrimonious – debate, powerful political pressures eventually forced the almost total abandonment of the CAA's key recommendations, leaving British Airways virtually unscathed. A small number of

Above:

A staggering investment of £2.5 million a week in one of the largest and technically most advanced computer and telecommunication systems will help British Airways to keep abreast of developments in Engineering, Operations Control, Finance and Materials Management.

British Airways/Adrian Meredith

route exchanges with British Caledonian had little effect either on profits or on the overall balance. The way ahead for British Airways was now clear, although it took another two years before the offer for sale of shares came to fruition. It must be said, however, that this procrastination could not be put at the airline's door.

Rush for British Airways Shares

Under the offer for sale in the UK, with separate offerings in the USA, Canada, Japan and Switzerland, 720 million Ordinary Shares of 25p each, competitively priced at 125p per share, were offered on 27 January 1987, valueing the airline at £900 million. With a number of successful flotations of public companies in the months immediately before, doubts were voiced about the timing of this particular issue. In the event, the overwhelming response took even British Airways by surprise, and the hefty premium above the offer price, even before trading officially started, laid the government open to the charge of having sold the airline on the cheap. Nearly 1.1 million applications were received, causing severe rationing. Even without the very large applications from institutional investors, the level of oversubscription was still almost 11 times.

Thought at one time as not an issue for 'the man in the street', the average final allocation was only 250 shares of which 47% went to employees and the general public, 36% to City institutions, and 17% to institutions abroad. The latter is still well below the overall limit of 25% for non-UK ownership. The power to impose such a limit was written into the Articles of Association in order to safeguard the Rights of British Airways to operate, particularly on international routes. There is always a danger that the bi-lateral agreements with certain countries could be placed in jeopardy if the airline ceased to be substantially owned and effectively controlled by UK nationals. Realistically, anything up to 35% would possibly be acceptable before intervention was deemed necessary. Until 1992, the maximum holding of any individual or connected group of persons, is limited to 15%. One encouraging aspect of the sale was the fact that British Airways employees emerged as enthusiastic applicants for the shares, receiving pre-ferential treatment with priority applications met in full for up to 25,000 shares. This, combined with other special offers, means that staff now own nearly 10% of the airline's equity. Mr John Moore, Transport Secretary, professed himself delighted that '. . . the public has placed such faith in this great British company.'

The New Marketing Organisation

Since the merger of BOAC and BEA in 1972, many organisational changes were implemented within the new British Airways which to the casual observer must have seemed, due to their frequency, like trial and error exercises. All were built around a regional structure which, although expedient at the time, has now been discarded in favour of a more functional approach, tending towards increased central control. This, it is hoped, has created the right environment for the achievement of more efficient overall performance levels. There is no doubt that privatisation of the national airline has not only shaped current thinking, but has considerably hastened its implementation. The massive success of the flotation bears out the validity of this philosophy.

The fundamental change from a regional to a highly functional type of marketing organisation was put into operation in September 1986, with the main objective of making the airline more competitive, to enhance its worldwide selling ability and to take it further along the way towards its ultimate goal of being the best and most successful airline in the world. The new structure is built around the teams that served British Airways for the previous three years, headed as before by Director of Marketing, Jim Harris, who joined the airline straight from school in 1947.

It is made up of seven precise functional units – World Sales, Customer Services, Strategy, Products/Brands, Marketing Services, Tactical and Yield Control, and Distribution and Systems – each led by a Senior General Manager. The World Sales Management team also includes Regional and District Managers, and reporting directly to the General Managers in Customer Services are Regional and Airport Managers. The separate business centres of Cargo, Tours, Poundstretcher and Travicom remain virtually unchanged from those set up in July 1983.

World Sales was established to fulfil a purely sales function, divorced from any other responsibility, to more easily direct sales performance towards maximum profitability for British Airways. In a major departure from previous thinking, British Airways is capitalising further on its extensive worldwide route network by not only selling seats from and to the UK, but also by encouraging travellers to fly British Airways from Europe to the rest of the world, from Africa to the USA, from Scandinavia to Australia, promoting its unmatched Heathrow hub as the gateway to the world – from all over the world. Selling the whole range of British Airways services is a £4 billion a year business, and the World Sales team relies heavily on 'Tactics' – the engine room of the new organisation – for information and direction on where to concentrate its efforts to produce the best overall result. Tactics' responsibilities extend to pricing, performance analysis and yield control, as well as the function of scheduling and resultant cost implications.

Other units with a vital role to play in selling for British Airways are Products and Brands, the creative 'think-tank' responsible for specific products such as Club World and Club Europe, Super Shuttle and Concorde, together with future developments; Marketing Services which look after advertising and promotion, customer relations and market research; and, of course, Customer Services. Although responsibilities are clearly defined, there are many local areas around the world where both Customer Services and Sales roles are filled by the same person. Even where this is not the case, everybody is expected to 'sell' the airline at all times.

Spearheading the airline's drive towards operational excellence and a consistent and superior level of service to that of its competitors, is the Customer Services team, which incorporates 15,000 British Airways staff across the world. They include all those working for Ground Operations London at the Heathrow and Gatwick terminals and their counterparts at other airports; people employed in reservations and travel shops worldwide; and the British Airways representative management personnel in each country where there is an office. In general terms, this means everyone who comes in direct contact with people outside the airline, be they customers, government representatives, aviation authorities or the like. There is also a central unit, based at Heathrow, to support the team around the world, and a 'quality' branch to set the standards and ensure they are being met. Training too comes under Customer Services.

Strategy's prime function is the short/medium and long-term planning, for up to 10 years ahead. It aims to predict future traffic and competition to enable the airline to be ready at all times and to respond quickly to any changes in the operating environment.

Finally, Distribution and Systems focuses on the design of medium and long-term programmes for British Airways' marketing business and the necessary support systems. The new structure is now well in place and beginning to make an impact.

A Final Look Ahead

The events of the last few years have, perhaps, exceeded even British Airways' own hopes and predictions, but what will the future hold for the airline as the 20th century comes to a close?

Progress may not be quite as dramatic but there is every confidence that demand for airline services will grow at a rate which is at least equal to that of economic activity in the parts of the world served. Now that the airline is in private hands, the way in which the UK government will implement future civil aviation policy will be an important factor. At the very least, British Airways will have to expect increased competition, but it hopes that its resources and position as one of the world's leading airlines and the largest by far in the UK, will enable it to successfully meet the challenges ahead. Wherever possible, it will develop existing services and embark on new routes when economically viable and where licences can be obtained. Opportunities for growth will perhaps be most pronounced within Europe, and the EEC in particular, where greater liberalisation of the regulatory frame-work winds its inevitable, if slow and tortuous path, towards a brighter horizon.

However, in common with other airlines, British Airways is susceptible to external factors such as sudden changes in economic and political conditions, competitive and regulatory environments, fuel prices and last but not least, to the volatility of foreign exchange rate markets, which can have a significant effect on results. It is difficult, if not impossible, to predict any or all of these, but the wide spread of British Airways' route network and range of ancillary services should offer some protection against unforeseen downturns in demand. Record orders for new aircraft throughout the industry during 1986, 1987 and so far in 1988, with a strong predominance of the 150-seater, may point to less uncertainty about passenger traffic growth than that experienced in recent years.

The most dramatic developments will take place in the air cargo business. The major operators have almost unanimously predicted that the market for world air cargo, currently worth about £15 billion, will grow to £37 billion by 1995. The critical area is the door-to-door premium segment which will have high growth rates and overtake the traditional cargo markets in revenues (£26 billion versus £11 billion). The premium freight market will, therefore, increasingly rival in revenues the passenger business. It is from this area where the main competition to the scheduled carriers will emerge in the form of mega express companies and small air courier operators who will offer both a full product range and total geographical coverage. British Airways has, however, one big advantage. By capitalising on its inherent major strengths such as its worldwide route system and hub capacity, it will be able to optimise the traffic mix on its routes and profitably involve itself in all market segments.

By 1990, British Airways will be flying the Boeing 747-400 with nonstop payload capability to link world hubs, with the exception of Europe/Australia. The manufacturer claims that even this should be possible by the turn of the century with the new prop-fan jets. The combination of enhanced payload capability and increasing use of Combis, will ensure that the British Airways scheduled long-haul services will meet all business passenger and premium cargo needs for the foreseeable future.

Perhaps the final word should be left to Chief Executive Colin Marshall: 'We have made great strides in creating an airline that offers the best service in the world – now we are going all out to win the glittering prize: that of the undisputed Best Airline in the World.'

Appendix A
The British Airways Fleet (as at 30 September 1988)

As befits one of the world's leading airlines, the British Airways fleet consists of a carefully evaluated blend of modern aircraft tailored to suit its varied activities and wide-ranging route system. It ranges from small turbop- rops to the supersonic Concorde and incorporates a number of types of varying capabilities and passenger capacities.

Airbus Industrie A320

European multi-national short-medium haul airliner which made its maiden flight on 22 February 1987. A highly- advanced, all-new twin-engined 150-seat aircraft, it was originally ordered by launch customer British Caledonian, but entered service directly with British Airways on 29 April 1988. The A320 is currently scheduled on a number of prime European routes and to North Africa.

Registration	Type	Serial		Date of delivery
G-BUSB	A320-100	(006)	Isle of Jersey	31. 3.88
G-BUSC	A320-100	(008)	Isle of Skye	3. 6.88
G-BUSD	A320-100	(011)	Isle of Mull	22. 7.88
G-BUSE	A220-100	(017)	Isles of Scilly	due 11.88
G-BUSF	A320-100	(018)	Isle of Man	due 89
G-BUSG	A320-100	(039)	Isle of Wight	due 89
G-BUSH	A320-100	(042)	Isle of Jura	due 89
G-BUSI	A320-100	( )	Isle of Anglesey	due 90
G-BUSJ	A320-100	( )	Isle of Sark	due 90
G-BUSK	A320-100	( )	Isle of Guernsey	due 90

BAe/Aerospatiale Concorde

Joint Anglo-French supersonic airliner, the only one of its kind currently in commercial service. Powered by four Rolls-Royce/SNECMA Olympus 593/610 turbojets giving a speed of more than twice the speed of sound, it first flew on 2 March 1969 and entered service with British Airways on 21 January 1976 to Bahrain. The 100-seat Concorde is presently scheduled to New York, Washington and Miami, but is also used extensively on charter work.

Registration	Type	Serial	Date of delivery
G-BOAA	Concorde 102	(206)	14. 1.76
G-BOAB	Concorde 102	(208)	24. 9.76
G-BOAC	Concorde 102	(204)	13. 2.76
G-BOAD	Concorde 102	(210)	8.12.76
G-BOAE	Concorde 102	(212)	20. 7.77
G-BOAF	Concorde 102	(216)	12. 6.80
G-BOAG	Concorde 102	(214)	6. 2.80

BAe ATP

The British Aerospace ATP (Advanced Turboprop) is an economic 64-72 seat short-haul aircraft, derived from the successful 748 and equipped with the latest in engine, propeller, flight deck and systems design. Eight of the type, which first flew on 6 August 1986, have been ordered by British Airways for use by the Highlands Division. Delivery will commence in November 1988 and be completed by the following summer.

Registration	Type	Serial	Date of delivery
G-BTPA	ATP	(2007)	due 11.88
G-BTPC	ATP	(2010)	due 12.88
G-BTPD	ATP	(2011)	due 1.89
G-BTPE	ATP	(2012)	due 2.89
G-BTPF	ATP	(2013)	due 3.89
G-BTPG	ATP	(2014)	due 3.89
G-BTPH	ATP	(2015)	due 4.89
G-BTPJ	ATP	(2016)	due 4.89

The ATPs will be named after Straths, which are wide valleys in the Highlands of Scotland.

BAC One-Eleven

Twinjet, short range airliner family which made its flying debut on 20 August 1963. The stretched 99-seat 500 Super One-Eleven was developed to a specific BEA require- ment and entered service with the state corporation in winter 1968. Also in service are several of the earlier and smaller 79-seat 400 Series. Both are powered by Rolls-Royce Spey 512-14 turbofan engines. One-Elevens are scheduled on domestic routes and to some European destinations.

Registration	Type	Serial		Date of delivery
G-AVGP	111-408EF	(114)	County of Nottinghamshire	4. 4.70
G-AVMH	111-510ED	(136)	County of Cheshire	11. 6.69
G-AVMI	111-510ED	(137)	County of Merseyside	1. 4.69
G-AVMJ	111-510ED	(138)	Strathclyde Region	21. 8.68
G-AVMK	111-510ED	(139)	County of Kent	13. 9.68
G-AVML	111-510ED	(140)	County of Surrey	4.10.68
G-AVMM	111-510ED	(141)	County of Antrim	22.10.68
G-AVMN	111-510ED	(142)	County of Essex	15.11.68
G-AVMO	111-510ED	(143)	Lothian Region	22.11.68
G-AVMP	111-510ED	(144)	Bailiwick of Jersey	4.12.68
G-AVMR	111-510ED	(145)	County of Tyne and Wear	2. 5.70
G-AVMS	111-510ED	(146)	County of West Sussex	10. 1.69
G-AVMT	111-510ED	(147)	County of Berkshire	23. 3.69
G-AVMU	111-510ED	(148)	County of Dorset	19. 3.69
G-AVMV	111-510ED	(149)	Greater Manchester County	10. 4.69
G-AVMW	111-510ED	(150)	Grampian Region	13. 4.69
G-AVMX	111-510ED	(151)	County of East Sussex	20. 6.69
G-AVMY	111-510ED	(152)	County of Derbyshire	9. 7.69
G-AVMZ	111-510ED	(153)	County of Lancashire	12. 8.69
G-AWBL	111-416EK	(132)	County of Leicestershire	12. 2.71
G-AWYR	111-501EX	(174)	County of Suffolk	ex B.Cal
G-AWYS	111-501EX	(175)	County of Norfolk	ex B.Cal
G-AWYT	111-501EX	(176)	County of Gwynedd	ex B.Cal
G-AWYU	111-501EX	(177)	County of Avon	ex B.Cal
G-AWYV	111-501EX	(178)	County of Powys	ex B.Cal
G-AXJK	111-501EX	(191)	County of Hereford	ex B.Cal
G-AXJM	111-501EX	(214)	County of Durham	ex B.Cal
G-AXLL	111-523FJ	(193)	County of Yorkshire	ex B.Cal
G-AYOP	111-530FX	(233)	County of Humberside	ex B.Cal
G-AZMF	111-530FX	(240)	County of Northumberland	ex B.Cal
G-AZPZ	111-515FB	(229)	Dumfries of Galloway Region	ex B.Cal
G-BBME	111-401AK	(066)	County of Shropshire	9. 4.74
G-BBMF	111-401AK	(074)	County of Worcester	30. 7.74
G-BBMG	111-408EF	(115)	County of Gloucester	10.10.73
G-BGKE	111-539GL	(263)	County of West Midlands	3. 3.80
G-BGKF	111-539GL	(264)	County of Warwickshire	12. 6.80
G-BGKG	111-539GL	(265)	County of Staffordshire	15. 8.80
G-BJRT	111-528FL	(234)	County of South Glamorgan	ex B.Cal
G-BJRU	111-528FL	(238)	County of West Glamorgan	ex B.Cal

HS 748

Short range twin turboprop which started life as an Avro project in 1958 and made its first flight on 24 June 1960.

Two versions are currently in service with British Airways, the 748-2B with 'hot and high' Rolls-Royce Dart 536s and the latest 2B Super, which incorporates engine hush kits and other significant improvements. The 748, fitted out for 44 passengers, is used by British Airways Highlands Division.

Registration	Type	Serial		Date of delivery
G-ATMJ*	748-225	(1593)	Glen Nevis/Gleann Nibheis	1. 3.82
G-BCOE	748-287	(1736)	Glen Livet/Gleann Lionhaid	10. 7.75
G-BCOF	748-287	(1737)	Glen Fiddich/Gleann Fithich	9. 9.75
G-BGJV	748-287	(1768)	Glen Avon/Gleann Athfhinn	10. 1.85
G-BGMN†	748-234	(1766)	Glen Finnan/Gleann Fionain	7. 6.86
G-BMFT†	748-266	(1714)	Glen Isla/Gleann Ile	4. 4.87
G-BGMO†	748-234	(1767)	Glen Goyne/Gleann Goinn	22 5.86
G-BOHY‡	748-2B	(1784)	Glen Shee/Gleann Sidhe	10. 3.88
G-BOHZ‡	748-2B	(1785)	Glen Turret/Gleann Turraid	10. 3.88
G-HDBA	748-287 Super	(1798)	Glen Esk/Gleann Uisge	13.12.84
G-HDBB	748-287 Super	(1799)	Glen Eagles/Gleann Eagais	14 12.84
G-HDBC‡	748-2B	(1786)	Glen Dronach/Gleann Dronach	20. 6.88

* Leased from Dan-Air
† Leased from Euroair
‡ Leased from DLT

Boeing 757

Advanced medium range subsonic airliner, powered by two wing-mounted Rolls-Royce RB211-535C turbofans. It made its first flight on 19 February 1982 and entered service with British Airways in February 1983. The type is scheduled between Heathrow and continental destinations and also serves the UK cities of Belfast, Aberdeen, Edinburgh, Glasgow and Manchester. Seating is provided for 180 passengers on international flights and for 195 on the Super Shuttle.

Registration	Type	Serial		Date of delivery
G-BIKA	757-236	(22172)	Dover Castle	29. 3.83
G-BIKB	757-236	(22173)	Windsor Castle	3. 2.83
G-BIKC	757-236	(22174)	Edinburgh Castle	9. 2.83
G-BIKD	757-236	(22175)	Caernarvon Castle	11. 3.83
G-BIKF	757-236	(22177)	Carrickfergus Castle	29. 4.83
G-BIKG	757-236	(22178)	Stirling Castle	27. 8.83
G-BIKH	757-236	(22179)	Richmond Castle	19.10.83
G-BIKI	757-236	(22180)	Tintagel Castle	2.12.83
G-BIKJ	757-236	(22181)	Conwy Castle	10. 1.84
G-BIKK	757-236	(22182)	Eilean Donan Castle	2. 2.84
G-BIKL	757-236	(22183)	Nottingham Castle	1. 3.84
G-BIKM	757-236	(22184)	Glamis Castle	22. 3.84
G-BIKN	757-236	(22186)	Bodiam Castle	24. 1.85
G-BIKO	757-236	(22187)	Harlech Castle	15. 2.85
G-BIKP	757-236	(22188)	Enniskillen Castle	13. 3.85
G-BIKR	757-236	(22189)	Bamburgh Castle	2. 4.85
G-BIKS	757-236	(22190)	Corfe Castle	1. 6.85
G-BIKT	757-236	(23398)	Carisbrooke Castle	2.11.85
G-BIKU	757-236	(23399)	Inverary Castle	8.11.85
G-BIKV	757-236	(23400)	Raglan Castle	10.12.85
G-BIKW	757-236	(23492)	Belvoir Castle	8. 3.86
G-BIKX	757-236	(23493)	Warwick Castle	15. 3.86
G-BIKY	757-236	(23533)	Leeds Castle	29. 3.86
G-BIKZ	757-236	(23532)	Kenilworth Castle	15. 5.86
G-BMRA	757-236	(23710)	Beaumaris Castle	2. 3.87
G-BMRB	757-236	(23975)	Colchester Castle	25. 9.87
G-BMRC	757-236	(24072)	Rochester Castle	22. 1.88
G-BMRD	757-236	(24073)	Bothwell Castle	29. 2.88
G-BMRE	757-236	(24074)	Killyleagh Castle	23. 3.88
G-BMRF	757-236	(24101)	Hever Castle	13. 5.88
G-BMRG	757-236	(24102)	Caerphilly Castle	1. 6.88
G-BMRH	757-236	(24266)	Norwich Castle	due 3.89
G-BMRI	757-236	(24267)	Tonbridge Castle	due 3.89
G-BMRJ	757-236	(24268)	Old Wardour Castle	due .89
G-	757-236	( )		due .89
G-	757-236	( )		due .89
G-BPEA*	757-236	(24370)		due 3.89
G-BPEB*	757-236	(24371)		due 5.89
G-DJRC‡	757-217	(23895)	Braemar Castle	25. 4.88

* On order for Caledonian Airways
‡ Leased from Monarch Airlines

Boeing 747

Long range, large capacity airliner, popularly known as Jumbo jet, which first flew on 9 February 1969. British Airways services began on the London-New York route in April 1971. The 747-136 and the two leased 747-2B4Bs are powered by four Pratt & Whitney JT9D-7A engines, whilst the 747-236Bs have Rolls-Royce RB211-524D4 powerplants. Nineteen 747-436s are on order with RB211-524G engines.

Registration	Type	Serial		Date of delivery
G-AWNA	747-136	(19761)	City of Peterborough	22. 5.70
G-AWNB	747-136	(19762)	City of Newcastle	23. 5.70
G-AWNC	747-136	(19763)	City of Belfast	30. 6.70
G-AWND	747-136	(19764)	City of Leeds	1. 3.71

Registration	Type	Serial		Date of delivery
G-AWNE	747-136	(19765)	City of Southampton	7. 3.71
G-AWNF	747-136	(19766)	City of Westminster	15. 3.71
G-AWNG	747-136	(20269)	City of London	8. 9.71
G-AWNH	747-136	(20270)	City of Inverness	16.12.71
G-AWNJ	747-136	(20272)	City of Sheffield	21. 3.72
G-AWNL	747-136	(20284)	City of Nottingham	20. 4.72
G-AWNM	747-136	(20708)	City of Bristol	4. 5.73
G-AWNN	747-136	(20809)	City of Leicester	11.11.73
G-AWNO	747-136	(20810)	City of Durham	8.12.73
G-AWNP	747-136	(20952)	City of Portsmouth	7.11.74
G-BBPU	747-136	(20953)	City of Dundee	15. 3.75
G-BDPV	747-136	(21213)	City of Aberdeen	9. 4.76
G-BDXA	747-236B	(21238)	City of Cardiff	28. 7.77
G-BDXB	747-236B	(21239)	City of Liverpool	16. 6.77
G-BDXC	747-236B	(21240)	City of Manchester	23. 6.77
G-BDXD	747-236B	(21241)	City of Plymouth	5. 4.78
G-BDXE	747-236B	(21350)	City of Glasgow	28. 3.78
G-BDXF	747-236B	(21351)	City of York	25. 4.78
G-BDXG	747-236B	(21536)	City of Oxford	17. 6.78
G-BDXH	747-236B	(21635)	City of Edinburgh	27. 4.79
G-BDXI	747-236B	(21830)	City of Cambridge	6. 3.80
G-BDXJ	747-236B	(21831)	City of Birmingham	3. 5.80
G-BDXK	747-236B	(22303)	City of Canterbury	4. 5.83
G-BDXL	747-236B	(22305)	City of Windsor	14. 3.84
G-BDXM	747-236B	(23711)	City of Derby	25. 2.87
G-BDXN	747-236B	(23735)	City of Stoke on Trent	17. 3.87
G-BDXO	747-236B	(23799)	City of Bath	23. 4.87
G-BDXP	747-236B	(24088)	City of Salisbury	22. 3.88
G-BJXN	747-230B	(20527)	—	ex B.Cal
G-CITB	747-2D3B	(22579)	City of Norwich	ex B.Cal
G-GLYN	747-211B	(21516)	City of Perth	ex B.Cal
G-HUGE	747-2D3B	(21252)	City of Exeter	ex B.Cal
G-NIGB	747-211B	(21517)	City of Gloucester	ex B.Cal
G-BLVE#	747-2B4B	(21097)	City of Lincoln	1. 6.85
G-BLVF#	747-2B4B	(21098)	City of Lancaster	1.11.85
G-BMGS*	747-283B	(20121)	—	27. 4.86

Leased from Middle East Airlines Airliban
* Leased from Scandinavian Airlines System

G-BNLA	747-436	(23908)	City of London	due 3.89
G-BNLB	747-436	(23909)	City of Edinburgh	due .89
G-BNLC	747-436	(23910)	City of Cardiff	due .89
G-BNLD	747-436	(23911)	City of Belfast	due .89
G-BNLE	747-436	(24047)	City of Newcastle	due .89
G-BNLF	747-436	(24048)	City of Leeds	due .89
G-BNLG	747-436	(24049)	City of Southampton	due .89
G-BNLH	747-436	(24050)	City of Westminster	due .90
G-BNLI	747-436	(24051)	City of Sheffield	due .90
G-BNLJ	747-436	(24052)	City of Nottingham	due .90
G-BNLK	747-436	(24053)	City of Bristol	due .90
G-BNLL	747-436	(24054)	City of Leicester	due .90
G-BNLM	747-436	(24055)	City of Durham	due .90
G-BNLN	747-436	(24056)	City of Portsmouth	due .90
G-BNLO	747-436	(24057)	City of Dundee	due .90
G-BNLP	747-436	(24058)	City of Aberdeen	due .90
G-BNLR	747-436	(24447)	City of Hull	due .90
G-BNLS	747-436	( )		
G-BNLT	747-436	( )		

With the delivery of the 747-436s, the 747/136s are due to be renamed to avoid duplication, as follows:
G-AWNA *Colliford Lake*/-AWNB *Llangorse Lake*/-AWNC *Lake Windermere*/-AWND *Coniston Water*/-AWNE *Derwent Water*/-AWNF *Blagdon Lake*/-AWNG *Rutland Water*/-AWNH *Devoke Water*/-AWNJ *Bassenthwaite Lake*/-AWNL *Ennerdale Water*/-AWNM *Ullswater*/-AWNN *Loweswater*/-AWNO *Grafham Water*/-AWNP *Haningfield Water*/-BBPU *Virginia Water*/-BBPV *Blea Water*. Boeing 747-236Bs G-BDXA will be renamed *City of Peterborough* and -BDXH *City of Elgin*.

Boeing 767

Eleven 250-passenger Boeing 767-336s are on order for delivery between November 1989 and February 1992. Fifteen options are also held. Powerplant is two Rolls-Royce RB211-524H.

Registration	Type	Serial		Date of delivery
G-BNWA	767-336ER	(24333)	*Severn Bridge*	due 3.90
G-BNWB	767-336ER	(24334)	*Forth Bridge*	due 11.89
G-BNWC	767-336ER	(24335)	*Clifton Bridge*	due 12.89
G-BNWD	767-336ER	(24336)	*Humber Bridge*	due 12.89
G-BNWE	767-336ER	(24337)	*Tower Bridge*	due 2.90
G-BNWF	767-336ER	(24338)	*London Bridge*	due 2.90
G-BNWG	767-336ER	(24339)	*Chelsea Bridge*	due 3.90
G-BNWH	767-336ER	(24340)	*Brig O'Doon*	due 2.91
G-BNWI	767-336ER	(24341)	*Iron Bridge*	due 3.91
G-BNWJ	767-336ER	(24342)	*Southwark Bridge*	due 3.91
G-BNWK	767-336ER	(24343)	*Kew Bridge*	due 2.92

Boeing 737

Boeing's 'baby' first flew on 9 April 1967 and the advanced 737-236 entered service with British Airways in February 1980. A short range airliner with accommodation for 106 passengers, the 737-200 is powered by twin Pratt & Whitney JT8D-15A turbofans. The 737 serves domestic and regional European routes and is used by Caledonian Airways on IT-flights from Gatwick, Manchester and other provincial airports.

Registration	Type	Serial		Date of delivery
G-BGDA	737-236	(21790)	*River Tamar*	4.12.81
G-BGDB	737-236	(21791)	*River Tweed*	16. 2.80
G-BGDC	737-236	(21792)	*River Humber*	8. 2.80
G-BGDD	737-236	(21793)	*River Tees*	25. 2.80
G-BGDE	737-236	(21794)	*River Avon*	13. 3.80
G-BGDF	737-236	(21795)	*River Thames*	21. 3.80
G-BGDG	737-236	(21796)	*River Medway*	3. 4.80
G-BGDH	737-236	(21797)	*River Clyde*	14. 4.80
G-BGDI	737-236	(21798)	*River Ouse*	30. 4.80
G-BGDJ	737-236	(21799)	*River Trent*	7. 5.80
G-BGDK	737-236	(21800)	*River Mersey*	16. 5.80
G-BGDL	737-236	(21801)	*River Don*	9. 6.80
G-BGDN	737-236	(21802)	*River Tyne*	11. 6.80
G-BGDO	737-236	(21803)	*River Usk*	25. 7.80
G-BDGP	737-236	(21804)	*River Taff*	13. 8.80
G-BGDR	737-236	(21805)	*River Bann*	18. 9.80
G-BGDS	737-236	(21806)	*River Severn*	26. 9.80
G-BGDT	737-236	(21807)	*River Forth*	17. 3.80
G-BGDU	737-236	(21808)	*River Dee*	13.11.80
G-BGJE	737-236	(22026)	*River Wear*	21. 3.80
G-BGJF*	737-236	(22027)	*Loch Fyne*	7. 4.80
G-BGJG*	737-236	(22028)	*Loch Avon*	29. 4.80
G-BGJH*	737-236	(22029)	*Loch Loyal*	13. 5.80
G-BGJI*	737-236	(22030)	*Loch Shiel*	1.10.80
G-BGJJ	737-236	(22031)	*River Swale*	18.12.80
G-BGJK	737-236	(22032)	*River Cherwell*	10. 3.81
G-BGJM	737-236	(22034)	*River Ribble*	8. 4.81
G-BKYA	737-236	(23159)	*River Derwent*	29. 8.84

Registration	Type	Serial		Date of delivery
G-BKYB	737-236	(23160)	River Stour	28. 9.84
G-BKYC	737-236	(23161)	River Wye	9.10.84
G-BKYD	737-236	(23162)	River Conwy	26.10.84
G-BKYE	737-236	(23163)	River Lagan	2.11.84
G-BKYF	737-236	(23164)	River Spey	2.11.84
G-BKYG	737-236	(23165)	River Exe	7.12.84
G-BKYH	737-236	(23166)	River Dart	14.12.84
G-BKYI	737-236	(23167)	River Waveney	3. 1.85
G-BKYJ	737-236	(23168)	River Neath	29. 1.85
G-BKYK	737-236	(23169)	River Foyle	2. 2.85
G-BKYL	737-236	(23170)	River Ayr	23. 2.85
G-BKYM	737-236	(23171)	River Cam	2. 3.85
G-BKYN	737-236	(23172)	River Isis	22. 3.85
G-BKYO	737-236	(23225)	River Kennet	13. 4.85
G-BKYP	737-236	(23226)	River Ystwyth	26. 4.85
EI-BTW‡	737-2Q8	(21960)		1. 6.88
EI-BTZ‡	737-2U4	(22576)		26. 3.88

* Operated by Caledonian Airways
‡ Leased from Air Tara

Lockheed L1011 TriStar

Large capacity, medium range wide-body transport, which first flew on 17 November 1970. Power is provided by three Rolls-Royce RB211 turbofans, which includes the 22B model in the early TriStar 1, and 524Bs with increased thrust and other improvements on the 200 Series. Seating in the various models ranges from 216 to 393 passengers. The TriStar entered service with British Airways in early 1975, and is used to the Americas, the Middle and Far East and on high-density European routes.

Registration	Type	Serial		Date of delivery
G-BBAE*	L1011-1	(1083)	Loch Earn	19.10.74
G-BBAF	L1011-1	(1093)	Babbacombe Bay	7.11.74
G-BBAG	L1011-1	(1094)	Bridgwater Bay	21.11.74
G-BBAH	L1011-1	(1101)	Lyme Bay	24. 1.75
G-BBAI*	L1011-1	(1102)	Loch Inver	4. 2.75
G-BBAJ*	L1011-1	(1106)	Loch Rannoch	19. 3.75
G-BEAK	L1011-50	(1132)	Carmarthen Bay	23. 1.76
G-BEAL*	L1011-50	(1145)	Loch Moy	16.12.76
G-BEAM	L1011-50	(1146)	Swansea Bay	10. 2.77
G-BGBB	L1011-200	(1178)	Bridlington Bay	10. 3.80
G-BGBC	L1011-200	(1182)	St Andrews Bay	22. 4.80
G-BHBL	L1011-200	(1193)	Largs Bay	22. 9.80
G-BHBM	L1011-200	(1198)	Poole Bay	29.11.80
G-BHBN	L1011-200	(1204)	Bideford Bay	1. 4.81
G-BHBO	L1011-200	(1205)	St Magnus Bay	13. 4.81
G-BHBP	L1011-200	(1211)	Whitsand Bay	15. 5.81
G-BHBR	L1011-200	(1212)	Bude Bay	27. 5.81

* Operated by Caledonian Airways

McDonnell Douglas DC-10

Medium to long-haul wide-body trijet, powered by General Electric CF6-50C2 turbofans, which was first flown on 21 June 1972. Eight of this model were taken over from British Caledonian which had operated the DC-10-30 successfully since introducing it into service in 1977. With British Airways, it serves on routes to the USA, Africa and the Gulf.

Registration	Type	Serial		Date of delivery
G-BEBL	DC-10-30	(46949)	Forest of Dean	ex B.Cal
G-BEBM	DC-10-30	(46921)	Sherwood Forest	ex B.Cal
G-BHDH	DC-10-30	(47816)	Ben More Forest	ex B.Cal
G-BHDI	DC-10-30	(47831)	Forest of Ae	ex B.Cal
G-BHDJ	DC-10-30	(47840)	Glen Cap Forest	ex B.Cal
G-DCIO	DC-10-30	(48277)	Epping Forest	ex B.Cal
G-MULL	DC-10-30	(47888)	New Forest	ex B.Cal
G-NUIK	DC-10-30	(46932)	Cairn Edward Forest	ex B.Cal

Appendix B – Sixteen Year Results and Operating Statistics

Years ended 31 March	1973	1974	1975	1976	1977	1978	1979	1980	1981	1982	1983	1984	1985	1986	1987	1988
Results																
Scheduled Services																
Passengers and baggage (£m)	360.5	444.3	526.6	660.0	898.6	965.1	1,191.4	1,409.9	1,489.5	1,608.7	1,770.9	1,905.6	2,253.6	2,376	2,481	2,858
Revenue – freight and mail (£m)	75.4	89.5	106.1	105.7	138.0	148.3	167.6	192.5	202.7	181.8	186.7	207.8	252.5	268	265	287
Total Revenue (£m)	435.9	533.8	632.7	765.7	1,036.6	1,113.4	1,359.0	1,602.4	1,692.2	1,790.5	1,957.6	2,113.4	2,506.1	2,644	2,686	3,145
Total Airline Operations (including Airtours)																
Revenue (£m)	464.2	566.1	663.5	801.5	1,073.9	1,156.1	1,403.3	1,654.4	1,749.8	2,010	2,172	2,382	2,797	2,981	3,054	3,523
Operating expenditure (£m)	431.7	512.9	665.3	798.8	978.1	1,099.3	1,327.3	1,638.4	1,854.0	2,005	2,002	2,108	2,494	2,776	2,871	3,282
Operating result (£m)	32.5	53.2	(1.8)	2.7	95.8	56.8	76.0	16.0	(104.2)	5	170	274	303	205	183	241
British Airways Group																
Turnover (£m)	539	647	748	916	1,248	1,355	1,640	1,920	2,061	2,241	2,497	2,514	2,943	3,149	3,263	3,756
Profit before interest and tax (£m)	35.6	64.1	5.0	11.6	115.8	79.0	109.8	54.9	(69.9)	10.8	204	293.7	304	234	192	228
Statistics																
Scheduled Services																
Revenue passenger km (m)	21,881	24,803	24,171	27,280	30,143	29,751	36,366	42,144	40,076	38,521	36,394	34,206	38,386	41,344	41,356	49,123
Available seat km (m)	38,646	41,703	41,126	44,816	48,576	49,637	56,387	62,534	64,043	57,752	54,710	53,386	56,031	60,759	61,722	69,970
Tonne km – freight and mail (m)	778.7	855.9	840.2	807.4	856.4	974.1	1,048.7	1,167.3	1,160.8	1,034.9	985.5	1,122	1,292	1,356	1,444	1,793
Total revenue tonne km (m)	2,720	3,061	2,997	3,249	3,607	3,711	4,417	5,036	4,812	4,503	4,307	4,244	4,810	5,155	5,267	6,345
Revenue per passenger km (p)	1.65	1.79	2.18	2.42	2.98	3.24	3.28	3.35	3.72	4.17	4.87	5.57	5.87	5.75	6.00	5.82
Revenue per RTK (p)	16.0	17.4	21.1	23.6	28.7	30.0	30.8	31.8	35.2	39.8	45.5	49.8	52.1	51.7	52.1	49.6
Available tonne km (m)	5,168	5,528	5,388	5,856	6,233	6,408	7,164	7,797	7,930	7,147	6,786	6,699	7,275	7,956	8,141	9,427
Passenger load factor (%)	56.6	59.5	58.8	60.9	62.1	59.2	64.5	67.4	62.6	66.7	66.5	64.1	68.5	68.0	67.0	70.2
Break-even passenger load factor (%)	51.5	52.4	59.0	60.6	55.4	56.4	60.3	66.6	67.0	66.6	60.4	54.8	59.3	61.9	62.0	64.4
Overall load factor (%)	52.6	55.4	55.6	55.5	57.9	57.9	61.6	64.6	60.7	63.0	63.5	63.4	66.1	64.8	64.7	67.3
Break-even overall load factor (%)	48.9	49.9	55.8	55.3	52.5	55.0	58.2	64.0	64.5	62.7	57.8	55.2	58.2	59.5	60.4	62.2
Punctuality (% within 15 minutes)		76	81	80	79	64	65	68	81	78	84	84	85	82	81	80
Number of passengers carried (000)	13,272	14,361	13,349	13,792	14,510	13,370	15,768	17,319	15,918	15,231	14,635	14,206	15,951	17,016	17,276	20,169
Tonnes of freight and mail carried (000)	250.6	268.2	250.2	199.9	211.1	226.9	247.9	264.5	242.4	205.2	199.4	229	259	274	291	361
Total Airline Operations (including Airtours)																
Available tonne km (m)	5,779	6,077	5,832	6,247	6,555	6,793	7,557	8,153	8,243	7,522	7,208	7,194	7,837	8,601	8,751	10,083
Number of passengers carried (000)									16,978	16,695	16,344	16,241	18,397	19,681	20,041	23,230
Net Operating expenditure per ATK (p)	7.5	8.4	11.4	12.8	14.9	16.2	17.6	20.1	22.5	24.7	25.9	27.1	29.8	30.4	30.9	30.4
Average staff – airline activities	54,500	54,600	54,861	53,977	54,362	55,438	55,985	56,140	53,616	47,753	39,693	36,096	36,861	38,939	39,498	42,709
ATK per employee (000)	106.1	111.3	106.3	115.7	120.6	122.5	135.0	145.2	153.7	157.5	181.6	199.3	212.6	220.9	221.6	236.1

Appendix C
British Airways Aircraft
Dimensions and Characteristics

Type	Powerplant	Wingspan	Length	Height	Max take-off weight	Typical Seating
Boeing 747-136	4x203kN Pratt & Whitney JT9D-7A	59.6m	70.7m	19.3m	333,000kg	18SL/90J/258M
Boeing 747-236B	4x230kN Rolls-Royce RB211-524D4	59.6m	70.7m	19.3m	372,000kg	18SL/88J/258M 463Y
Boeing 747-236B Combi	4x230kN Pratt & Whitney JT9D-7J	59.6m	70.7m	19.3m	377,750kg	18SL/88J/110M/ 40 tonnes FR
BAe/ Aerospatiale Concorde	4x169kN Rolls-Royce/SNECMA Olympus 593-610	25.5m	62.14m	11.27m	185,150kg	100F
Lockheed L1011-1 TriStar	3x187kN Rolls-Royce RB211-22B	47.35m	54.34m	18.88m	195,050kg	198C/136M 393Y
Lockheed L1011-200 TriStar	3x222kN Rolls-Royce RB211-524B	47.35m	54.34m	18.88m	211,375kg	18F/60J/138M
Lockheed L1011-50 TriStar	3x187kN Rolls-Royce RB211-22B	47.35m	54.34m	18.88m	204,175kg	18F/64J/138M 393Y Airtours
McDonnell Douglas DC-10-30	3x234kN General Electric CF6-50C2	50.57m	55.45m	17.74m	259,457kg	18F/35J/180M
Airbus Industrie A320	2x112kN CFMI International CFM56-5A1	33.91m	37.57m	11.76m	66,000kg	152C or M
Boeing 757-236	2x166kN Rolls-Royce RB211-535C	38.05m	47.32m	13.56m	100,000kg	180M 195M (Shuttle)
Boeing 737-236	2x69kN Pratt & Whitney JT8D-15	28.3m	30.53m	11.28m	52,750kg 54,200kg	106M 128Y
BAC One-Eleven -400	2x50kN Rolls-Royce Spey 511-14	26.97m	28.5m	7.47m	40,000kg	79M
BAC One-Eleven -500	2x53kN Rolls-Royce Spey 512-14DW	28.5m	32.61m	7.47m	43,000kg	99M
HS 748-2B	2x1,700kW Rolls-Royce Dart 536-2	31.23m	20.42m	7.57m	23,150kg	44M
HS 748-2B Super	2x1,700kW Rolls-Royce Dart 536-2	31.23m	20.42m	7.57m	21,100kg	44M

F First Class   **C** Club Europe   **J** Club World   **M** Economy   **Y** Tourist   **SL** Sleeperseats   **FR** Freight

Appendix D
The Forerunners

Aircraft Transport and Travel Ltd
Founded 5/10/1916. First service 25/8/1919 London-Paris with de Havilland DH16. Ceased operations 17/12/1920, assets taken over by Daimler Hire Ltd.

Handley Page Transport Ltd
Founded 14/6/1919. First service 2/9/1919 London-Paris with Handley Page 0/400. Merged to form Imperial Airways Ltd 31/3/1924.

Instone Air Line Ltd (S. Instone & Co)
First service 13/10/1919 (private) and 18/2/1920 (public) London-Paris with de Havilland DH4/DH4A. Merged to form Imperial Airways Ltd 31/3/1924.

Daimler Airway (Daimler Hire Ltd)
First service 2/4/1922 London-Paris with de Havilland DH34. Merged to form Imperial Airways Ltd 31/3/1924.

British Marine Air Navigation Ltd.
Founded 23/3/1923. First service 25/9/1923 Southampton-Guernsey with Supermarine Sea Eagle. Merged to form Imperial Airways Ltd 31/3/1924.

Imperial Airways Ltd
Formed 31/3/1924 out of Handley Page Transport, Instone Air Line, Daimler Airway and British Marine Air Navigation. First service 26/4/1924 London-Paris with de Havilland DH34. Merged with British Airways Ltd to form British Overseas Airways Corporation (BOAC) 1/4/1940.

Hillman's Airways
First service 1/4/1932 Romford-Clacton with de Havilland DH80A Puss Moth and DH83 Fox Moth. Merged to form Allied British Airways Ltd 30/9/1935. Renamed British Airways Ltd 29/10/1935.

Spartan Air Lines Ltd
Registered 2/2/1933. First service 12/4/1933 Cowes-Heston with Spartan Cruiser. Merged to form Allied British Airways Ltd 30/9/1935. Renamed British Airways Ltd 29/10/1935.

United Airways Ltd
Registered 4/4/1935. First service 30/4/1935 Heston-Blackpool with de Havilland DH86 and DH89 Dragon Rapide and Blackpool-Isle of Man-Carlisle with Spartan Cruiser. Merged to form Allied British Airways Ltd 30/9/1935. Renamed British Airways Ltd 29/10/1935.

British Continental Airways Ltd
Registered 15/4/1935. First service 2/7/1935 London-Ostend-Le Zoute probably with de Havilland DH86. Absorbed by British Airways Ltd 1/8/1936.

British Airways Ltd
Registered 30/9/1935 as Allied British Airways from merger of Spartan Air Lines, Hillman's Airways and United Airways. Name changed 29/10/1935. Merged with Imperial Airways Ltd to form British Overseas Airways Corporation (BOAC) 1/4/1940.

British Overseas Airways Corporation (BOAC)
Established 1/4/1940 through merger between Imperial Airways and British Airways. Merged with British European Airways Corporation (BEA) 1/4/1972 to form the present British Airways.

Highland Airways Ltd
Founded 3/4/1933. First service 8/5/1933 Inverness-Wick-Kirkwall with General Aircraft ST4 Monospar. Merged to form Scottish Airways Ltd 12/8/1937.

Northern and Scottish Airways Ltd
Founded 21/11/1934. First service 1/12/1934 Renfrew-Campbeltown-Islay with DH84 Dragon. Known for a short time as Northern Airways Ltd before merger to form Scottish Airways Ltd 12/8/1937.

Scottish Airways Ltd
Formed 12/8/1937 out of Highland Airways and Northern and Scottish Airways. Became part of the Associated Airways Joint Committee (AAJC) 5/5/1940. Taken over by BEA 1/2/1947.

Railway Air Services Ltd
Founded 21/3/1934. First service 7/5/1934 Plymouth-Haldon-Cardiff-Birmingham-Liverpool with de Havilland DH84 Dragon. Became part of AAJC 5/5/1940. Taken over by BEA 1/2/1947.

Blackpool and West Coast Air Services Ltd
Founded 3/4/1933. First service 22/6/1933 Blackpool-Liverpool-Isle of Man with DH84 Dragon. Name changed to West Coast Air Services Ltd at end of 1937.

West Coast Air Services Ltd
Until late 1937 known as Blackpool and West Coast Air Services Ltd. Became part of AAJC 5/5/1940. Ceased 29/6/1946. Technically to BEA 1/2/1947.

North Eastern Airways Ltd
Formed 4/3/1935. First service 8/4/1935 London-Leeds-Newcastle with Airspeed AS6 Envoy. No operations at start of war. Technically to BEA 1/2/1947.

Olley Air Service Ltd
Formed 10/1/1934. First service 13/7/1935 Croydon/Brighton-Deauville with de Havilland DH84 Dragon. Became part of AAJC 5/5/1940, but no scheduled services at the time. Technically to BEA 1/2/1947.

Isle of Man Air Services Ltd
Registered 21/1/1935. First service 27/9/1937 Liverpool-Isle of Man with de Havilland DH89A Dragon Rapide. Owned jointly by Olley Air Service, LMS Railway and Isle of Man Steam Packet Co. Became part of AAJC 5/5/1940. Taken over by BEA 1/2/1947.

Channel Air Ferries Ltd
Formed as subsidiary of Olley Air Service 8/5/1936. First service 23/5/1936 Brighton/Ryde with Short S16 Scion. Routes transferred to Great Western & Southern Air Lines Ltd 3/12/1938, but operated until 3/1939.

Great Western & Southern Air Lines Ltd
Formed 3/12/1938 to take over GWR and SR-sponsored routes of Railway Air Services Ltd and routes of Channel Air Ferries Ltd. Became part of AAJC 5/5/1940. Taken over by BEA 1/2/1947.

Western Isles Airways Ltd
Formed 12/8/1937 jointly by Scottish Airways Ltd and David MacBrayne Ltd. Services operated by Scottish Airways. Became part of AAJC 5/5/1940. Taken over by BEA 1/2/1947.

Air Commerce Ltd
Founded 1/12/1934. Services believed to have ceased by outbreak of war. Became part of AAJC 5/5/1940. Technically to BEA 1/2/1947.

Aberdeen Airways Ltd
Founded 2/1/1934. First service 11/9/1934 Aberdeen-Glasgow with Short S16 Scion and de Havilland DH86. Changed name to Allied Airways (Gandar Dower) Ltd 13/2/1937.

Allied Airways (Gandar Dower) Ltd
Formerly known as Aberdeen Airways Ltd. Did not become part of AAJC. Activities taken over by BEA 12/4/1947.

Jersey Airways Ld
Registered 9/12/1933. First service 18/12/1933 Portsmouth-Jersey with DH84 Dragon. Did not become part of AAJC. Services operated under the Channel Islands Airways name from 1/9/1945.

Guernsey Airways Ltd
Registered 24/11/1934. First service 9/6/1935 Guernsey-Jersey with Saunders-Roe Windhover. Did not become part of AAJC. Services operated under the Channel Islands Airways name from 1/9/1945.

Channel Islands Airways Ltd
Formed 1/12/1934 as a holding company for Jersey Airways and Guernsey Airways. Services operated under its own name from 1/9/1945 when owned by GWR and SR. Taken over by BEA 1/4/1947.

British Latin-American Air Lines Ltd
Formed 1/1944 but did not start operations before a change of name to British South American Airways Ltd 10/1945.

British South American Airways Ltd/Corporation
Formerly known as British Latin-American Air Lines Ltd. First service 15/3/1946 London-Lisbon-Bathurst-Natal-Rio-Montevideo-Buenos Aires with Avro Lancastrian. Became a State corporation 1/8/1946. Absorbed by BOAC 30/7/1949.

British European Airways Corporation (BEA)
Established 1/1/1946 as a division within BOAC and became a separate State corporation 1/8/1946. Took over the services of the Associated Airways Joint Committee (AAJC) 1/2/1947. Merged with BOAC 1/4/1972 to form the present British Airways.

Cambrian Air Services Ltd/Cambrian Airways Ltd
Formed 25/4/1935 as charter operator with de Havilland DH60 Gipsy Moth. First service 5/1948 Cardiff-Weston-super-Mare with de Havilland DH89A Dragon Rapide. Renamed Cambrian Airways Ltd 23/5/1955. Became part of British Air Services, a subsidiary of BEA, on 1/10/1967. Continued operations under own name until its integration into British Airways 1/4/1972.

BKS Aero Charter Ltd/BKS Air Transport Ltd
Formed 7/2/1952 as a charter operator. First service 18/5/1953 West Hartlepool-Northolt with Douglas DC-3. Changed name to BKS Air Transport Ltd late 1953. Became part of British Air Services 1/10/1967. Changed name to Northeast Airlines Ltd 1/11/1970.

Northeast Airlines Ltd
Formerly known as BKS Air Transport. Absorbed into British Airways upon its foundation 1/4/1972.